May Excitement Follow You Everywhere

by

James Nibb

DORRANCE
PUBLISHING CO
EST. 1920
PITTSBURGH, PENNSYLVANIA 15238

Dorrance Publishing Co
585 Alpha Drive
Suite 103
Pittsburgh, PA 15238
Visit our website at *www.dorrancebookstore.com*

ISBN: 979-8-8860-4325-9
eISBN: 979-8-8860-4594-9

Introduction

During my career, I have been a technical advisor to power plants and fuel suppliers around the world. All the stories are true; only the names of the characters involved have been changed to protect their identity. Many are funny, some are risky, none are boring.

The title, *May Excitement Follow You Everywhere*, is an ancient Chinese curse. In Confucian philosophy, order, peace, and tranquility were the accepted ideals. Excitement was regarded as disorder and anybody causing excitement was cursed.

The world has changed dramatically in the last fifty-five years. Many social norms of that era are now unacceptable. Burning coal has been deemed an environmental disaster, but the well-being of most countries would never have developed without coal. Underground coal did not disturb the surface to a great extent, but today, great swathes of tropical rain forests are being burned to make way for surface mining of low-quality coal.

In my mind, the greatest destroyer of the planet is the chainsaw. This technology has allowed forests to be cut down hundreds of times faster than in the nineteenth century with no skill or interest in conservation. Everything that breathes exhausts greenhouse gases!

Fossil fuels will have to be part of the fuel mix in the future, even though the largest production of electricity will be from wind and solar. Batteries are a long way from being major stores of electricity and taking even thirty minutes to recharge a car battery every 300 miles is going to severely limit electric road transportation. Geothermal, hydrogen, and liquid air storage will not be widely available until far in the future, if ever. Hydro has its own draw-back; look at the geopolitical confrontation in Ethiopia and Egypt. Assuming electric power and light will have to be available 24/7, new fossil fired power plants will have to be funded and built, even though they may only operate for 10% of the hours in a year. The energy thirst, of an ever-increasing world population, will never be satisfied by renewables alone.

During the last forty-five years, I have travelled to all corners of the globe. I have visited most countries, some multiple times, and some over twenty-five times. For years, I flew over the Atlantic or Pacific Oceans *every* weekend. There were many dull and boring flights. However, some routes were always wild for one reason or another. The flights from New York to Calgary always had their share of riotous behavior, as had the route from Hong Kong to San Francisco. The low-cost airline flights from the UK (especially Luton) to Bulgaria, most of which most were late evening affairs, sometimes had as many as half the plane full of drunks even before taking off, with open invites to young ladies on the flight to join the 'Mile High Club.'

I have been extremely fortunate in not having any major criminal incidents (although many 'near misses'). I got robbed on the Paris metro and had difficulty getting another driving license and credit cards as well as withdrew $20,000 (covered by VISA) in the fifteen minutes before I could cancel the cards and report the theft to the police. I also got mugged in Bulgaria with a headbutt and had all the same things stolen again, but I suppose the worst case was when I just sat in my car and a police officer jumped on me, gave me a breath test, and I lost my driving license for three months. More about that later.

I was sexually attacked only once at a youth hostel in Ilkley, England, but I was able to fight off the attacker. I have to say, it left me with an unhappy feeling towards gays. I also avoided an attack by thirty or so women on Shrove Tuesday (Mardi Gras) as a young apprentice. I had to go lifting equipment testing at a company where ninety percent of the employees were women, and it was a long-standing British tradition (banned long ago but not stamped out completely) that women would sexually attack apprentices on Shrove Tuesday. My company realized the problem late and sent a protection squad to extract me from a small elevator where I was besieged, but I got out unharmed.

Growing up, I had no other prejudices. I treated girls, boys, rich, poor, stupid, intelligent, just the same, regardless of nationality, race, color, and religion. I did recognize there was prejudice all around me, but I did not like bullies and kept well clear of them.

Chapter 1: Early Life

I was born in Accrington, an industrial town in Lancashire, England. The town is in a very wet part of England, where it is said that the most beautiful girls have webbed feet.

My birth was during the so-called 'phony war', just after the start of the second world war. It was called phony as there was little or no land action following the invasion of Poland before the threat of invasion and bombing of British cities. My mother went into hospital at the start of labor for a C-Section, but our doctor was not available, so a German doctor began the operation. He pulled out my sister and was about to sew up my mother when he reached in and pulled me out. My father danced round the hospital with joy (as nobody believed my mother was expecting twins) and decided to call me the same name as my brother, who had died in infancy a few years before. I am sure I am not unique, but I have two birth certificates and a death certificate!

I do not remember much about the war. We were reasonably comfortable, considering it was war time, and only four bombs were dropped on our town during the whole war. I had no relations fighting in Europe, but two uncles were officers in the Indian army who fought in Burma (now Republic of the Union of Myanmar) against the Japanese. We had food rationing till I was eight years old: children received one glass of orange juice each week.

My father had a reserved occupation, as well as having poor eyesight and severe hay fever, which meant he was not called up for military national service, so he was at home during the whole war. He had to do fire watching at one of the local village railway stations, working till 5:30 pm, then home till 10 pm, fire watching till 6 am (although sleeping in a local mill), and home again for breakfast before going back to work at 8:30 am. Just before the end of the war, I went with him on a few occasions and slept in the mill.

I started school full-time at three years old in the infant school at the top of our street. At age seven, we were moved up to the elementary school, also at the top of our street. The school had a good academic record, and it was the same school that my father had gone to. He was one of the first students at the school immediately after it was built, and my father's name was on a board in the main hall for graduating top of his class—which came back to haunt me.

For a part time during the war, we had a trainee missionary from Ghana staying at our house. She was treated like one of the family and often took my sister and I on long walks and shopping in the town. We were very fond of Florence.

In the elementary school, I was not allowed to be in the same class as my sister, as there was a school rule that twins could not be in the same class. Our parents went crazy about this as the school was 'streamed,' with my sister going into the top class and me into the lower class.

When she was two to four years old, my sister suffered from numerous illnesses with continuous problems of a lazy eye and weak bones, and she was frequently in hospital. The nurses insisted on her reading at an early age, so she could read long before I could. I never had any illnesses except for measles, tonsil removal, and a protective appendectomy.

I had a misspent youth, being more interested in sport and travel than serious study. Things were never normal for me. I had no friends in my school class, but made some friends older and younger than me, and some from different schools including private schools. We played soccer every moment we had free and anywhere where there was space: the school playground, parks, even garbage dumps and street corners. We used anything we could find as a ball, from soccer balls, basketballs, tennis balls, and even tin cans when we had nothing else.

I loved to travel, and even as young as seven years old I travelled on brickwork trucks some weekends, but mainly during school holidays to nearly all the power plants being built at that time. The drivers did not object to having me around, especially in winter as driving through the major cities like Manchester were invariably blanketed in smog as thick as pea soup. At times it was so thick I had to walk in front of the truck with a bright red jacket on to ensure the truck stayed on the road.

At elementary school I was not very happy. Almost as soon as I got there, I was accused and found guilty of throwing an apple three hundred feet and breaking the window of a passing bus. Everyone found it incredible that I, aged seven, could manage such a feat, but the principal hauled me out in front of the whole school, and I was fined five dollars by the police. This was a large fine for a young schoolboy in those days. When you get a name, it sticks with you.

The school had an exceptionally good reputation, but at that time I found that at least the older boys were vicious, anti-Semitic, and very pro-German. The few Jewish boys in the school were tied to the school rails, insulted, and had tomatoes thrown at them. This was unbelievable to me, as the horrors of Nazi Germany were being shown on the news. This was not the experience later at this school, as it certainly was not known for being anti-Semitic, but also there were few if any Jewish children at the school later.

This was 1947, and soldiers were coming back from the war, bringing German wives and their adopted children with them. The children, speaking no English, looked absolutely petrified when coming to the school for the first time, but could not believe it when they were treated like heroes and heroines. Again, I too found this quite unbelievable.

My cousin was the music master at the school, and he took a delight in punishing me, especially when singing. He was brutal with his own children, too. He would stand in front of me with his ear almost in my mouth and listen for any wrong note, at which time he would drag me out by my ear and make me sing the whole song repeatedly in front of the class.

As a boy, I sang soprano and was encouraged—sometimes forcibly—by my cousin to sing solo at music festivals. At one of the biggest music festivals for the whole region, the adjudicator got up and said, "Your singing is particularly good, but I never want to see you again. You make me sick!" I had a habit of swaying in time to the music, which at that time was a no-no.

We had some sadistic teachers. One, if you did anything wrong would say, "Face the east and bow to Allah," and you had to bow and say, "Allah, the giver of all good gifts." When you bowed down, he would hit you on the backside with his shoe. If you did not face east, he would hit you repeatedly until you bowed to the east. That punishment was handed out to both girls and boys.

I had quite a regimented upbringing during my time at junior school, but this was typical of British families at that time. Monday was our washing day, and we would help in the evenings making beds and so on. Most evening had some activities; Tuesday was Cub Scouts at the Cannon Street Baptist Church school in the center of town. Wednesday was elocution lessons with Miss Wooler. Thursday was soccer after school, and Friday was Fish Chips and Manchester Caviar (mushy peas), a real highlight of the week.

Saturday mornings we went to the Odeon Cinema for young people's cinema with a sing-along, and usually a Western cowboy film. Saturday afternoon was PROFESSIONAL SOCCER. My dad took me either to watch the town team in the third division north, Accrington Stanley, if they were playing 'at home,' or to Burnley some six miles away, who were in the first division. We went with my father's 'girl friends' the Miss Hindles: Mable, Mary, Muriel, and Myra. We took along a folding step so I could be as tall as them and watch the games.

Saturday evenings were spent in reviewing the football results for the day and attending church social events or amateur dramatic performances, which both my parents performed in. Some of the plays were riotous. In one memorable show, my mother was in bed with my uncle when he lost his false teeth under the sheets, and the audience killed themselves laughing.

Sunday morning was church, and the afternoon consisted of Sunday School, roast beef, and Yorkshire pudding, followed by church again in the evening. I sang in the choir. No football was allowed that day.

From the age of five to thirteen years old, our holidays were always spent at Fleetwood, a small seaside town thirty miles away. It was the nearest seaside resort we could get too due to my father's acute hay-fever; he was a basket-case during the summer and spent all his time in bed after work. The first visit was just after the war ended, and I always remember the railway station at Kirkham where we changed trains being full of German prisoners of war in the process of being sent back to Germany. At Fleetwood every morning there was a procession of trawlers heading to Iceland with an equal number returning. We played soccer and cricket on the beach, and I sailed my model yacht on the boating lake and even played golf where you could hire left-handed drivers and putters, as I am left-handed. Summer holidays at Fleetwood were always great.

Chapter 2: Secondary School

Just before I was eleven years old was the dreaded 11+ School Examination. The 'Eleven Plus' examination was at eleven years of age and the result was used to decide which secondary school you would go to. The top school was the grammar school or high school, the second was the technical school, and the lowest was the so-called 'secondary modern' school. I really did nothing to try to pass! My parents tried to encourage me to study and give me 'carrots,' but to no avail. The day after the 11+ Exam, my mother took me to Preston Railway Station where I went wild watching famous trains while she froze in the waiting room at the station.

The dreaded results day came, and my sister passed... but I failed! My parents and I were devastated. They decided on two possible courses of action: one, take the examination for a fee-paying school (Blackburn Queen Elizabeth's Grammar School, six miles away from home) or two, send me to the secondary modern school in Accrington. I sat the Queen Elizabeth's Grammar School exam and passed, but looking at the finances, my parents considered it not the best use of money. They decided I should sink or swim at the secondary modern school.

On my first day at the Hyndburn Park secondary modern school, they put me in the lowest grade class, also known as the 'C Stream.' I was amongst the dunces, arsonists, and other derelict youths.

But miracles will happen. I woke up and said, "This is not the place for me."

I was really helped by my form teacher who taught PE and Geography, and who also played soccer for the town's soccer club, Accrington Stanley. He was my real hero! He gave me a job, although it was most unusual for any student to get a specific task, and I kept this job for the whole four years at this school. The job allowed me to be in school at any time of the day or night, gave me access to the headmaster's office, and let me use the school telephone at any time. It also kept me out of control of the prefects, who could issue 'disorder marks.'

We, like all English secondary schools, had prefects. In English schools, prefects were twelve pupils selected by the principal from the senior class to keep discipline in the school. The prefects could issue disorder marks, and three disorder marks resulted in corporal punishment from one of the teachers. Each teacher had different forms of punishment. My PE teacher hit students with the running shoe, our science teacher used the cane, the principal used the crocodile strap, but the worst was the woodworking teacher. He used a T-square chalked at the end and hit you until all the chalk was on your trousers. In all my time at the school, I only got hit once, when the whole class was hit by the T-square for simply not lining up in a straight line.

The job I got was the school metrological officer. My job was to forecast the weather at the school for that day and the next. I got tremendous freedom, which nobody else in the school had. I frequently left school and went to Oak Hill Park where the town metrological office was. I was able to phone all the local contacts concerning the weather, even the BBC metrological service. I searched the school and found old instruments, bought new ones, and set up anemometers, barometers, hydrometers, sunshine gauges, rain gauges, and so on. Nine other people in the town, most of them retired professionals, read their instruments at the same time and plotted them on a town map. We were each given an extra daily task. I had to draw the barometer isobars and pressure gradients for the town and deliver this information to the central observatory office.

The only thing I did not like about this Physical Education/Geography teacher was he also had a bit of a brutal attitude. Every Wednesday afternoon, we had to go cross-country running, and the last two to arrive back at school, always got a beating. We also had to swim the canal on the way back, and anyone who could not swim had to run an extra two miles to the nearest bridge—and naturally, they were the ones that always got a beating. If the canal was frozen, we could all just slide over the ice and the non-swimmers did not get a beating. We were 'allowed' to have a cold shower when we got back to school.

At the end of the first six months, I was promoted to the B Stream, and the end of the first year, promoted again to the A Stream. I ended up at that school being a prefect, house captain and—for the final year—school Head Boy.

In my life outside school, as well as playing soccer, I was interested in trains and ships. Often, I took the train to Preston for 'trainspotting' on the main Glasgow to London line watching for eight hours or more. My greatest pleasure was visiting Liverpool docks, often traveling by overhead railway. On one occasion, I managed to climb and hide inside a stanchion on the quay side when the burnt-out Empress of Canada was being lifted upright.

I later applied and got a permit to visit any British-owned dockyard and take photos of any ship other that Royal Navy ships, but that led me into trouble.

In my mid-teens, I went on a holiday with my parents to Cypress, on our first-ever trip out of the United Kingdom. At that time, Cypress was a British dependent territory. I went down to the docks and photographed an Israeli navy ship and was unceremoniously arrested by two Israeli Navy ratings and thrown in the brig. They thought I was an Egyptian spy, and I was made a prisoner of war. I could not stop laughing. Me, a fourteen-year-old prisoner of war!

My parents got involved, as did the local politicians, police, and the Royal Navy. After much discussion, and ultimately opening the camera to expose the film, I was allowed to leave. The ship was a former Royal Navy frigate which had just been sold to the Israeli Navy and re-flagged the INS Eilat, a few days before. Sad to say, shortly after, the ship was sunk by an Egyptian missile and lost with all hands.

I wanted to join the Merchant Navy as a deck officer, but my parents were dead against it—and rightly so, as there were very limited shore opportunities if I got bored of the sea. They persuaded me to go into engineering, with the idea that at twenty-one years old I could make a choice: stay on land, or go to sea, with a qualification which allowed me to do both. My parents encouraged me to start evening courses in science and engineering subjects, as well as extra-curricular studies in English, Mathematics, and Physics.

So began my long life of evening study from the age of thirteen… to the age of thirty-four, believe it or not! Twenty-one years of study! I studied chemistry from a book and carried out experiments in my uncle's back shed, as he was a chemist, and I just took the O level high school leaving examination without ever attending any school classes in chemistry. I was not, however, allowed to carry out any chemical experiments at home.

At age ten, I joined the St. John's Ambulance Brigade (an organization much like the Red Cross) as a cadet after witnessing and assisting at a serious accident, which had a lasting impression on me. A boy of my age was run over by a bus right in front of me and had to have his leg amputated while under the bus. I was small enough to get under the bus while the doctor and medics had great difficulty. He was bleeding profusely so they had no time and were not able to move the bus without causing further injury. Helping an amputation was traumatic, and I had nightmares afterwards for some time. My mother came screaming as she thought it was me trapped under the bus.

I rose to the rank of sergeant in the ambulance brigade and was in line for a commission, but then got distracted.

The funeral service part of our family needed a bagpiper at some funerals and gave me a practice chanter (a practice instrument, not as loud as the pipes and no bag but with the same notation and sound). They encouraged me to learn the bagpipes with the ambulance brigade pipe band.

The Accrington St. John's Ambulance Brigade had a pipe band, the oldest non-military pipe band in the world (founded 1864) and I joined it, practicing in their drill hall as I was banned from playing at home. I bought a set of fully ivory-mounted bagpipes from the band. My set of pipes were made in South Africa of ivory, silver, and African black wood and were reputed to have been played at the battle of Megersfontein in the Boar War of 1899. The pipe band had an affiliation with the Cameron Highlanders Regiment and were given their old uniforms and pipes when they bought new ones. I still have those pipes but now use a more modern concert-pitched set. After a year on the practice chanter, I could play the required fifty-six tunes as well as dance the *Fling* and *Seann Trubhas* Highland dances. My favorite tunes were "Colonel Robertson," also called the "Massacre of Glencoe" when played slow and used in the film *Last of the Mohicans*, and *Leaving Port Askaig*. I then practiced often with the marching band and played at two events, but night school and other activities limited my involvement.

Chapter 3: On Stanley On

I still played soccer whenever I could, not that I was good at it, but I started having knee cartilage problems. The doctors could not help, but a chiropractor got my knee back in shape twice. After the third time I was told, "Give up football and start cycling." At that, my father decided to buy me a new touring bicycle.

The bicycle was not like a modern-day mountain bike made of light-weight alloy with twenty-four gears. This bike had a hub dynamo, and a four-speed, Sturmey-Archer hub gear changer with side panniers, and when it was fully loaded, I could not lift it off the ground.

My Sunday School teacher said, "Hey, why not cycle to a Stanley away match?" and recommended that I look at cycling the 240 miles round-trip to Darlington. He was a friend of Les Cocker, a Stanley player and later coach of the English team which won the world cup in 1966. This needed a great deal of planning. Up to then, I had not cycled more than 30 miles in a day. The earliest I could leave was Friday at 4:30 pm, and I needed to get to Darlington soccer ground by Saturday at 2:30 pm. In between was a range of hills calling the Pennies. I decided to spend Friday night at a youth hostel in Stainforth some fifty miles away, and then attempt the Pennies first thing Saturday morning. All went well, but by Saturday at lunchtime I was feeling weak and tired and was still twenty miles from Darlington. Somehow, I managed to keep going, but by the time I got to the soccer stadium in Darlington I was beat.

Les Cocker found me and invited me into the changing room and have a bath before the match. I had never been in the dressing room of a professional soccer team before. At Darlington, there were no showers, just a fifteen-foot diameter, three-foot-deep bath with hot soapy water. At the end of the match, eleven hot sweaty bodies jumped into the bath. Stanley lost 2-0, but the team would not hear of me cycling back and took me to dinner at Scotch Corner Hotel, then took me and my bicycle back to Accrington on the coach.

I was a keen Accrington Stanley Soccer Club supporter before that, but after Darlington, I cycled to all the soccer stadiums in the old third division north of the soccer league. Even the 260 miles in total, there and back, to 'British West' (as it was called by soccer supporters) Hartlepool, and 280 miles to Gateshead, could be done in a weekend with difficulty, as well as Wrexham, Mansfield, Carlisle, Derby, and other far-flung 'corners of the empire.'

On one trip, I went to Birkenhead (across the River Mersey from Liverpool) to watch Tranmere Rovers play Accrington Stanley. My great aunt and uncle lived with their three daughters only a few miles from Prenton Park, the Tranmere Rovers soccer stadium. After the match, their daughter Illis asked me if I wanted to go to hear an up-and-coming skiffle group at some club (maybe the Cavern) in Liverpool. I had never heard of the up-and-coming group called The

Quarrymen (who later became the Beatles), but I went along anyway. I must admit, I was not too thrilled in the crowded, noisy, smokey atmosphere. The music was good but just like any other skiffle group with guitars, a washboard, and a tea chest as bass. Fancy electronic gear or double basses were not affordable at the time.

The journey to Gateshead was really challenging. First the Pennine chain, a ridge of hills, had to be crossed. Then there was nowhere to stay five hours cycling distance from home, most of it up-hill, or requiring a short detour and adding to the distance. The places to stay were also inhospitable. Garsdale Head some fifteen miles off track and required the negotiation of a farm track all in the dark and cold. I had to carry my bike over steppingstones at the head of the river Wharfe, leave the bike in a chapel, collect the key from the dark lonely chapel, and tramp up hill to unlock the deserted youth hostel.

In the morning, I repeated the procedure but a least from there to Gateshead it was mostly downhill or flat. Getting there by two-thirty was a challenge, and the only time to eat was during the game at Gateshead. The team gave me a ticket for the director's enclosure, and I sat next to the most famous British children's and adult's comedian, Ken Dodd, who presented awards to children at half time.

Then came the next challenge: leaving at five o'clock to get to Barnard Castle youth hostel by 9:30 in the evening, after which time nobody was allowed in. I peddled up the many 'banks,' as they called hills in that part of the world. Then Sunday it was back over the Ribblehead summit and home, exhausted.

When they changed the soccer leagues from third division north and south to none-geographical third and fourth divisions, I lost interest after a trip to Coventry City, which was 330 miles round-trip. I could not make it back by Monday morning and got in serious trouble. All other third or fourth division clubs south of Coventry were completely out of reach.

Night school classes were invariably on a Wednesday night, when Stanley played under the floodlights, so it was rare that I watched any games on Wednesday night and missed some of the key games, like when Stanley played Blackburn Rovers in front of 17,000 spectators.

Chapter 4: My Career

This was all well and good, but the major issue was a career. My father had some influential friends, namely Sir Oliver Simon of Simon Carves Ltd, and Harrod Moore of Imperial Chemical Industries (ICI). They decided that the best course of action was an indentured graduate Engineering Apprenticeship at the company Foster, Yates and Thom Ltd, Heavy Precision Engineers and Boiler Manufacturers, Blackburn, established in 1826. My fate was sealed.

On leaving school, I became a mechanical engineering apprentice in their so-called indentured student engineer program. Myself, my father, and numerous people from the company had to sign and attach their waxed seal to the agreement with a formal signing. The agreement had phrases like, "*The student apprentice will not gamble with cards or dice or frequent taverns.*"

The program allowed me to have at least one day off a week to go to college, which supplemented my two nights per week evening classes. Sometimes I had two days a week at college, but to do that, I had to work all day Saturday, meaning two days study and two nights with four days' work.

I really did learn a lot, some of it good, others not so good. I spent three to six months in every type of work associated with heavy engineering and boiler manufacture: fabrication, turning, machining, fitting, marking-out, toolmaking, chain testing, X-ray testing, inspection, planning, and design. I learnt about the 'us and them' attitude, and how not to advance with the times. I wanted to learn electric arc welding and X-ray inspection of welds, but the factories act stipulated nobody under eighteen years old was allowed to weld and carry out X-ray inspection. The first four months in the fabrication shop was when I was seventeen years old with the last two months being over eighteen, so I was able to weld parts of a power plant X-ray and carry out nondestructive and destructive testing of the test coupons of my own welds.

In the boiler shop, the gantry crane driver had a box of small rivets in his cab, and any time a member of the management entered the boiler shop he was met by rivets raining down on him. "Oops, sorry, the bag must have opened accidentally," shouted the crane driver. Most of the boiler shop workmen were stone deaf and communicated with hand signals. It was noisy, hot, dirty work, but they were very skilled and never used any measuring device, just a piece of chalked string. Much to the annoyance of management and the company's police force, they always managed to be in the local pubs by three o'clock in the afternoon.

At that time, they were still manufacturing the same boiler designs they made in the nineteenth century, most of which were sold to India. Although the rest of the works modernized, they had mixed success. Throughout the four years I was a student apprentice, on average I studied for eighteen hours, and worked for twenty-four hours each week. Sometimes it was twenty-two hours per week of study. I also studied technical German and Nuclear physics as additional courses. During the summer, I got two weeks' vacation on the exact same dates every year but had to work all the rest of the summer.

Most of the time in the fitting and erection shop, I worked on torpedo tubes for both frigates and submarines, and therefore did not have to do military service, being deferred until I was twenty-one. By that time, compulsory military service was abolished. As most of the fitters were big men and had difficulty climbing inside torpedo tubes, I got the dirty *deafening* work of being inside the tubes when the fitter tested the rivets on the brass runners, and the tubes rang like a bell!

The frigate tubes had to be test-fired when completed, which was normally done one tube at a time, but the navy commander who came to the test decided to fire all six tubes at the same time, which lifted the roof off the building. Fortunately, the roof dropped back in almost the same place! I was sheltering inside a partially finished torpedo tube when that happened.

The management were good, but fond of their women. Some of their secretaries were not just secretaries but also 'sleeping companions,' with the offices having a special place, nicknamed The Chateau of Shame, which the management could book for an evening or all night. The management had their own toilet which had a sign on it: "This is where all the big Nobs hang out."

Most of my time in the heavy and light machine shops was spent assisting in setting up very large fabrications for machining. In the light machine shop, I assisted in setting up a lathe to machine the 50-foot-long, eight-inch diameter drive shaft for an electro-tinning line of a steelworks. Machining the shaft forging was very dangerous. As soon as a cut was made, the shaft would spring almost out of the lathe stays and chuck. I actually did productive work in the milling department with a milling machine on my own. The person on the milling machine next to me played trombone in a local band and he gave me the music, and he imitated the trombone part while I imitated the clarinet part as we worked. I used to practice my bagpipes inside the boilers being built in the boiler shop.

Chapter 5: Social Activities

My two-week summer vacations were spent touring Scotland. It was remarkable that I went there every summer for four years, as during the first visit it rained none-stop for the last twelve days of a fourteen-day holiday. I spent many happy hours at railway waiting rooms, drying off as they all had roaring coal fires. The evenings made up for everything with Scottish country dancing every night at the various youth hostels.

At seventeen years old, all the people I had played football with decided on a change of direction. It was time to meet the opposite sex, much to the scorn of my sister. We all enrolled in the Acadian School of Ballroom Dancing. We were taught the quickstep, foxtrot, and waltzes and thrust into the arms of reluctant girls.

From there, we graduated to Christ Church Youth Club to more modern music and dancing bop. I met my first girlfriend there and had a great time. After four months there, we graduated to the Conservative Club Ballroom, the premier dancing establishment in the town. To get tickets, we had to dash from the Stanley match and line up for tickets as, by six in the evening, all the tickets would be gone. She and her parents were also fanatical Stanley supporters. We danced to Chicago and Manhattan Spiritual, and at home to Pat Boone records. In my eyes, she could never do anything wrong, but she ran off after nine months for a younger person, leaving me broken-hearted, although I could not, even then, ever criticize her. We did not see one another often, but when we did, we were too embarrassed to talk. We met again some fifteen years later and are still good friends.

Just at that time, I did my mandatory six-months design office experience in the Admiralty drawing office, but nearly got the sack for lack of attention to detail. In the end, maybe it was for the best as I got back to some serious studies.

During this time, as well as going to college on day release and night school two nights a week, I started to go to German night classes. Our teacher was a German Jewess who escaped Germany in 1934, as her husband was a captain in the British army. She had a mixed reception in Accrington and my grandfather was not too fond of her, as in 1937 she had set up the British-Soviet Friendship Society. Even so, she was a good teacher. She and her whole family had been interned in a camp during the summer of 1940 until the summer 1945. We spent the first six months of her class 'getting to know Germany,' and she had us singing folk songs and telling funny stories. She brought in grammar gently and encouraged us to have pen friends at her former school in Konigswinter on the Rhine. I was "allotted "the daughter of the English teacher in Konigswinter, and we became great friends all her life. Both of our families spent many summer holidays together.

My first trip to Germany with our class, we went to a restaurant with our class and the girl's school class. In Germany, high schools only finish their *arbitur*-final exam, when they are nineteen years old. I was told to ask for the waitress. I knew that waiter was 'Herr Ober,' but did not remember what waitress was. Then I remembered my grammar: In German, you add '-in' to make it feminine. So, I shouted out, "Oberin!" at which all the girls split their sides laughing. I had addressed the waitress as Mother Superior!

We were invited to an evening at the home of the Roman Catholic school chaplain, and Herr Kaplan introduced me to his mother saying, *"Ich Mochte gern vorstellen, Herr Nib."* (*I would like to introduce you to Mr. Nib*). The old lady said, *"Herr Was?"* (*Mr. What?*) Herr Kaplan repeated it, and she again said, *"Herr Was?"* After the third time she said, *"Oh sehr angenhame Herr Holtzworm,"* at which all the girls burst out laughing. She had called me Mr. Woodworm!

Chapter 6:
A Fully-Fledged
Design Engineer

At the end of my apprenticeship in 1961, I was a designer in the drawing office and a graduate member of the Institution of Professional Mechanical Engineers. I worked with a great bunch of people, working on power plant condensers and feed heaters. We used slide rules and log tables—I bet young people today don't even know what they are—to calculate stresses, pressures, and flow. I left two years later to join the nuclear power industry as a budding design engineer.

At this time, I spent all my holidays, summer, and Christmas in Germany and Switzerland, always having a great time with my German girlfriend and her family. We had a fabulous time in Zermatt, although I could not eat the raw meat that they eat and got quite sick.

Soon after that, I started in the nuclear industry with six weeks' vacation, plus ten statutory days' holiday, making eight weeks in total—the longest vacation I have ever had in my life! As my design office was a long way from home, I got a travel allowance. I also bought a Fiat 1100 car, a real passion wagon, where the front bench seat would move completely to the dashboard and the backrest folded down to make a double bed! I took the ferry to France and drove to Germany to meet my longtime girlfriend. I realized when I got there that she had given me up for dead for joining, in her view, the hated nuclear industry.

I got a real shock at work, as I was expected to be able to write computer programs in basic and run intricate calculations. There were some two hundred lines of input followed by three hundred lines of calculations and a toilet-roll length of output. It was a real struggle, but fortunately my fellow assistant was a dab hand at it with four years of experience. Our lead engineer was a different story. Mean, nasty, uncouth, and with little knowledge at all, he took to blaming everyone else for his mistakes. He was from the Gorbals, Glasgow, had a real chip on his shoulder, and was altogether a nasty person. On the bright side, my job did allow me to sit and pass the confidential civil service technical German translators exam.

It was a life of extremes. One part working on computer programs for real problematic engineering issues, and then three months with three others designing a quarter inch diameter nut and bolt! When the first batch of two hundred were made, they were all wrong and had to be scrapped. Finally, we got it right and had to be on hand at the reactor while our nut and bolt was live tested.

I was invited to a dinner dance at Windscale, Cumbria (the site of the first nuclear power plant and both military and civil research). I took a girlfriend who was from Accrington and a German teacher at Harris College, now Preston University. At the dance, my girlfriend was invited to sit with the other women at one side of the dance floor, while at the other side the men were propping up the bar.

Afterwards, she made it clear that she wanted nothing to do with that organization or me, as all the engineers' families lived in an isolated secure compound. All the women could talk about was money, and who could and who could not afford what, as they all pulled out their little books which told them how much every person was earning.

At that event, we got in trouble for getting our instructor drunk. The next morning, he promptly fell off the reactor loading rig and was in hospital for six months.

Our office had a field hockey team, and I was invited to join. I had never played field hockey before but learned reasonably quickly. The team played in a league comprised of a few company teams, but most were university or college teams. My first league game was my last! We played in Liverpool against Mount Pleasant College, a teacher training college. In field hockey, each team supplies an umpire. We had an umpire but Mount Pleasant only had a female umpire available. In reality, the match should have been cancelled, but as we had travelled a hundred miles to the game and there were three hundred or so students and teachers from Mount Pleasant there to watch, our umpire and captain accepted the lady umpire. She knew the ladies' field hockey rules but was unfamiliar with the rules for men's hockey, which are different.

Our captain, who was our goal tender, got more and more furious. There was talk about abandoning the match halfway through. During the break, there were more discussions but also beer drinking, especially on the part of our captain. Ten minutes further into the game, their umpire gave an incorrect foul against our goal-keeper captain, and he turned round and hit her in the face (accidentally I am sure) with his hockey stick.

Run for your life! The Mount Pleasant team and spectators chased us off the pitch, and we were lucky to get to the changing room without being beaten up. This was 4 pm, and still at 6 pm there were thirty or forty people trying to batter down the door. By 10 pm there were only six people, and by eleven we finally sneaked out to our waiting coach for the journey home.

Some of my colleagues at work played the bagpipes with the Clan Stewart Pipe Band, mainly at Blackpool, a famous seaside resort. They asked me to play, as they were inundated with requests for performances. They had signed a contract which was particularly onerous. The Queen's Theater had a variety show in July, August, and September with famous comedians, acts, dancing girls, and choruses. At the end of each performance, they had a Highland scene with singers and dancers *and* the pipe band, who had to enter marching and playing down the steep aisles between the audience, playing the tune "Road to the Isles," of all things.

The pipe band was contracted to play for fifteen minutes each performance, one at 7:45 pm at the end of the first show, and 9:45 pm at the end of the second show, six nights per week. There was also a Saturday matinee performance with at least six pipers per show. This was really tough, as we had to drive like crazy from work to be at the theatre at 6:30 pm at the latest, and could not leave till 10:30 pm at the earliest. It meant the whole band was locked in playing six nights a week and all-day Saturday.

The first week was fun, as it involved mixing with the chorus girls, singers, and well-known British comedians like Ken Dodd and Morcombe and Wise. We were not allowed to leave the theatre between 8 pm and 9:45 pm, being in kilt, sporran, plaid, and so on. By the end of the first week, we knew all the comedian's gags, all the chorus girls, and every minute of the show.

The second week, band members started to sneak out at 8 pm, mainly to a local bar. With everybody inebriated at the bar, girls invariably tried to find out what the band members were wearing under the kilts and provided free drinks as incentives. The early performance went off as normal, but the second was usually a disaster. It was difficult to negotiate the steep aisles. Marching down them in the dark was very difficult during the first performance, but marching down them the second performance, especially after a few or more drinks was... chaotic. On the third evening of the second week, the bass drummer went head-over-heels over his big bass drum, with his legs and kilt open to all. The audience went wild. They thought it was all part of the performance. The bass drummer was rushed into hospital, and from then on, only one two pipers took part in the highland scene.

I played solo at a few New-Year's Eve parties for the band, and a Christmas Macy's-type parade but called it a day.

At work, after a year, they refused to grant me full civil service acceptance, so I applied for the position as a general assistant engineer in the national electricity generating company. All the people in the atomic energy thought I was mad. Giving up a job for life, at least eight weeks' vacation every year? But the pay prospects were better.

I soon learned the electricity industry method of job interviewing, which was very formal, but every interview was to some degree different. The standard practice was to appear before a panel of between six and twelve people who would all ask questions.

In my interview for my first job at a power plant, I was asked if I had any questions before the panel of twelve people asked me questions. I asked, "Is this an experimental power plant, as it is not in operation at the moment?" Those were the only words I said in the interview. All twelve people nearly fell of their chairs!

Each took fifteen minutes to tell me, "Oh no, this is a production plant, but we're having difficulties which we want you to help with." At the end they said, "Oh my god, we have used all the time up and have five more *candidates* to interview." I got the job!

Much to my great surprise, and the power company's surprise, the nuclear company insisted I give six months' notice. Fortunately, the power company was a customer of the nuclear industry and both sides agreed on three months' notice. The stupid thing about it was the nuclear company gave me exciting and challenging work for those last three months.

Chapter 7:
My First Power Plant

The plant was really two separate plants, an A plant with 1930s equipment and even a 1920s triple expansion steam engine, an old ship's engine. This part of the plant should have been shut down, but, at the time I joined, there was a massive demand for electricity which was not being met by the building program.

On first entering the electricity supply industry I had to attend various orientation courses. One of them was the mandatory first aid course with an examination at the end of it. I had already taken this course and had an up-to-date pass of the examination. However, I was still ordered to go to the hospital to take the course. At the hospital, they accepted my course result and, as the course was over-subscribed, they asked me to go on another course instead. The only course available at that time was a *MIDWIFERY* course, so I went and learnt how to deliver babies and even delivered one myself! Back at the power plant they announced that I had successfully completed the course and jokingly stated I was always there to assist in the delivery if ever one occurred at the power plant. As there were three women pregnant at that time at the power plant, they were not too thrilled at the idea of a young engineer acting as midwife if one went into labor at work!

The B plant was only three years old, with bigger and more powerful units than the A plant. It had continuous problems as the plant had the only 'wet-bottom' boilers in the UK and was designed for a specific type of coal. Within the first year of start-up, the coal board closed the mine that supplied the coal. I spent most of the time at that plant trying to find and test substitute coals. It was a real fight to keep the units running.

Even the old A plant units were back in service, but none too reliable. Everybody mucked in. I did my own job during the day, and in the early evening I helped the operators keep clear the B station 'monkey holes' clear of molten slag. It was hard, hot, dangerous work. Every evening there was a call for maximum generation. After clearing the monkey hole at 5 pm, all the engineers gathered in the control room watching the frequency starting to fall. At lower frequencies than 50 Hertz (alternating current cycles per second in the UK verses 60 Hertz in the USA), we had to chop-off customers, mainly houses in certain districts, with more and more districts if the frequency kept falling, and ultimately stop the whole plant if it fell too far.

It was unnerving, as we knew people who lived in the houses we were cutting off. We all fought like crazy to keep the plant running, and there was no 'us and them' mentality at that time.

One afternoon, I visited the A plant control room. On my way back to B plant, I passed under the economizer of one of the old chain grate boilers. There was a mighty bang, and the whole plant became enveloped in dense steam and boiling hot water raining down everywhere. I was unable to even see my nose. I hid inside a stanchion, but it got hotter and hotter and boiling water on the floor was rising. I must admit, I started saying my prayers, as I thought it was the end. Finally, the boiling rain started to slow, and shortly after, the steam dissipated. I escaped, unharmed. This had also happened at another plant, and they were not so lucky; the people caught under it got scalded to death.

Unfortunately, later at that plant the 'us and them' mentality prevailed, as there were people working there who were the same workmen who I met during my apprenticeship. With great fanfare, the company developed a new slogan: "Inform and Consult." To launch it, they had commissioned a big banner. When they first unveiled the banner, some wag had already got to it and moved the "In" and "Con" to read "Conform and Insult."

Up to now, I had lived at home and commuted to work by car. I also had a girlfriend who also worked in the office at the power plant.

I had started work at that plant the same day as a head of department. He was a very dynamic person, and it transpired that his family were in the same business as my greater family, that of undertakers. He assumed I knew everything about the undertaking business and that I was a Freemason, so he often talked about Freemasonry, which was very useful later. He went on to be a power plant manager in Northern Ireland and was well known for taking a teddy bear to meetings and saying, "I am prepared to spend the night here if we have not concluded the meeting by tonight." He was too dynamic for some people and was later nicknamed "The Rat."

He and others encouraged me to apply for higher rank jobs in the industry. A few interviews were very discouraging, such as when I was on vacation in Switzerland, I was invited for interview at a nuclear power plant, only to be asked stupid questions like, "Can you row a boat?" Ahh. They had already decided who was going to get the job, and it wasn't me!

Chapter 8:
The Midlands Region

After two years, I applied for and got a higher position at a larger power plant. At the time, we were paid based not only on your position at the plant, but also the size of the power plant. An engineer at a large plant was paid the same salary as the plant manager at a small power plant. I moved up to an assistant planning engineer.

At this interview, all the candidates sat in the plant manager's secretary's office, and I soon realized that the secretary (a formidable lady, nicknamed Queen Bee) was carrying out the interview. The formal interview in front of a panel was just functional.

Queen Bee bestowed nicknames on everyone, and she gave me the name Squirrel, which I kept for the next seven years. She settled on this name because, in her view, I hid away valuable documentation.

My personal life got a shock as I now had to live somewhere else, and my girlfriend was a hometown girl. Her ancestor, five generations before, was Alice Nutter, who was one of the last people to be hung in England as a so-called Pendle Witch. She ditched me, as I now had to move some 140 miles to the Midlands.

My manager recommended that I go and live in Ridware Hall. Ridware Hall was owned by an ancestral couple who had hit harder times and took in paying guests, but still liked to assume they were landed gentry with a cook, house maid, butler, gardener, and so forth. The cook was built like a wrestler, and you did not argue with her. She had been married six times and three of her husbands died in mysterious circumstances. One was drowned on the top deck of a double decker bus which plunged into the river Trent, which was only five feet deep, with the cook and her husband in it. The cook got out okay!

I left home on the first of January 1967 and moved into an absolutely freezing room with ice on the inside walls of my bedroom in a turret of Ridware Hall.

The water quality there was not good. The ancestral old man frequently sprayed oil onto the water pump and into the well! They had a monster kettle and only poured water and tea leaves in, and just tea out. You could stand a spoon in the kettle and the spoon would never fall over.

At dinner the Bakewell Tart was so hard that we could fling it from a fork into the light fittings on the high ceiling.

At that time, miniskirts were all the rage, and we went around pubs measuring up miniskirts to ensure they met 'British Standards.' It amazing what these girls would let us do, even with their boyfriends watching.

At that plant, I had a great boss and people to work with. This plant suffered from severe corrosion, as the local coal was high in sulphur and chlorine. The first five years the plant had worked well, but by then you could simply push your figure through metal platework, so most of the work was replacing corroded sections but also finding more benign coals.

Being unmarried and having no girlfriend at the time—which I suspect made my bosses see me as expendable—I was hoisted up the outside of the 250 feet chimney to the top wearing a facemask and breathing gear and a heat-protective suit. With the chimney operating, I examined the twenty-foot high, cast-iron cap. I was horrified to find I could push my figure through the corroded bolts which were supposed to hold the cap together as they crumbled to dust. I got down from there like a scared rabbit. This was a big issue. To replace the cap, the whole station would need to come off-line, and it was winter, so the demand for electricity was high. The decision was to rope off the area and wait till summer to carry out the replacement.

Chapter 9:
Disastrous Vacations

During my time at that plant, I had two disastrous vacations. The first was a holiday on the Costa Brava, Spain, in late June. I travelled all day to get there on a very early morning train to London, then the morning flight from London to Perpignan, France, and then by coach to Tossa De Mar, a famous Spanish holiday resort. I arrived there at 4 pm and went straight to the beach in swimming gear, laid on the beach, and fell fast asleep.

I woke up at 9 pm, very badly burnt all over my torso and face. I could not put any clothes on for the pain and staggered back to the hotel. A young German lady saw me in the hotel reception and said, "Oh no, it's obvious what happened to you. You had better come to my room and lay on the bed while I go out and get some medication."

I was in agony. She put ointment on me every three hours throughout the night, and for the next three days and nights. She arranged liquid food and water for me. By the fourth night, I was feeling better and could sit up and eat a normal meal. By the sixth day, I got up and went outside. On the seventh day it was time for her to go home and I went back to my room for the first time. On the eighth day I went out to a folk concert, and to the beach on the ninth day, before heading home on the tenth day. I kept in touch with the German lady and took her to dinner on one of my trips to Germany. She was a really good Samaritan.

Later, I went for a skiing holiday to Austria with a colleague from the power plant. The first five days were good, although I am not a great downhill skier. I don't like the planks of wood on my feet. I am more happy ice skating. At a wild party on the fifth evening, I did not feel well, and by the time I got to the hotel, I was running a high fever and a pulse rate of 120. The hotel owner called the doctor, and the doctor sent my colleague out in the deep snow at 1 am to wake up the drug store owner and fill in my prescription for antibiotics and other medication. I was in bed the rest of the holiday and was quite ill on the way back to Ridware Hall. I had to stay in bed for a further two weeks, and then my colleague came down with the same ailment.

In the three years since I left the nuclear industry, my salary had doubled. Again, I was encouraged to apply for higher positions. I applied for the position of technical development engineer. During the interview at the headquarters for this job, they asked me what I thought of my boss and how difficult was it working for him. I did not fall for that trap, but I did not get the job either.

I studied law at night school for two years so that kept me busy although I did go dancing afterwards at the Top of the World Stafford. On weekends, I went with the Birmingham Intervarsity Club sailing on a large lake, and on the Irish sea at Barmouth, both in Wales. The Intervarsity Club was great fun and wild at times like hiking, part of it, nude up Cadre Idris (a mountain in Wales) in the snow. All that came to an end too soon.

Chapter 10: East Midlands

After another two years, following an interview, I was offered the job of planning and development engineer at another power plant with a higher salary. The power plant was fortunate in having very good reliable plant and a good quality fuel supply, although still high in sulphur and chlorine. The management of this plant had been very laid-back and really did not have much to do, except go every day for an extended lunch 'hydraulic testing,' as it was called, at the local pub and were very set in their ways.

The assistant planning and development engineer at the plant was very bitter about not getting the job. According to him, he had been promised by the management he would get the job. He refused to work for me and even refused to come to work. It was sad, because he was a good engineer, but the company, in the end, asked him to resign or he would be fired.

The power plant had new challenges, as there was a need for the plant to be on low load or shut down at night, which they had never done before. The company board decided to change the existing personnel and bring in new dynamic management (including me) to shake up the whole organization. They got a bigger shake up than they bargained for!

I left Ridware Hall in June of 1969. The first week in Newark-on-Trent was a big celebration for the plant winning the Good Housekeeping trophy. This trophy was awarded to the best station in the country for not only cleanliness, but efficiency and availability throughout the last year. The old management were invited along with the regional chairman, who was known to be rather sexually mischievous, 'randy' as it is called in the UK, but the new management oversaw this event. The event was also attended by most of the plant personnel and families, including teens over fourteen years old, and held at the plant's sports club, an old church in the center of town.

The new management decided to add a more risqué event than the usual singers. A nurse was invited from a Nottingham hospital, who we found out later was well-known for baring it all after a few drinks. At the end of the first half, the nurse came on stage and did a stripping act to a mixed reaction, but then danced off-stage and sat naked on the chairman's lap, who seemed to greatly appreciate the gesture.

At the interval, unbeknownst to everyone, the plant manager and deputy manager got a young electrical engineer inebriated and persuaded him to go up on stage in the second half to help undress the nurse. It started off well, with most of the audience egging him on, but the nurse had other ideas. As he removed one article of her clothes, she proceeded to remove one article of his clothes. At that point some of the audience, also intoxicated, became even wilder in their encouragement while others fell silent. When they were both naked, the nurse kneeled down, and started to give the engineer a blowjob. There were shrieks of horror from nearly all of the audience, but others still screaming encouragement. At the critical time, the nurse turned the engineer to face the audience and he ... over the people in the front row, just missing the chairman!

STONY SILENCE! A look of horror crossed over everyone's face, and seconds later the regional chairman got up and screamed, "Nobody saw that, it did not occur, you will all sign to that effect before you are allowed to leave this club." There and then in front of everyone, the manager and deputy manager were threatened with the sack if it became public knowledge, ordered to draw up a statement for the attendees to sign, and put a watch on the young engineer who by then realized what had happened and was uncontrollable.

During the next two days, the management team, including me, were dispatched to the homes of the employees to convince them not to go to the press or police. A day and night watch were put on the young electrical engineer.

Fortunately for everyone, nobody did go to the police or the press. The young engineer was instantly promoted and moved to a power plant at the other end of the country. The regional chairman was ultimately made of the chairman of the whole UK power company and given a knighthood. The manager and deputy manager were later made regional directors and the incidence forgotten until a year later.

At that time, there was only one computer in the region and that was at the regional headquarters. Occasionally I went to headquarters to run programs, but normally I just sent in the input data and got the results back at the power plant. I was working late one evening at headquarters trying to finish and get back to the power plant, when in rushed the regional chairman's personal assistant who ordered me to leave my work and follow him to the sports club. He asked me if I could play table tennis, as the regional chairman was visiting their sports center. The sports club was new and was to be officially opened the next day, and the regional chairman wanted to play table tennis, which the PA said he could not play. I was puzzled by this explanation.

In the new sports club, the table tennis table was set up, and there was the infamous regional chairman with the deputy chairman and the deputy's beautiful daughter, who introduced themselves to me. I was told to partner the deputy chairman while the regional chairman partnered his deputy's daughter. It was most embarrassing right from the start. On the first stroke, when the daughter leaned over the table, the regional chairman had his left hand up her skirt. I am sure there was steam coming from the deputy chairman's ears, and the daughter, after a few more shots, stopped and asked me to partner her. The chairman would not allow it and said we can swap sides in a few minutes. I am sure he realized they would both walk off if he carried on, so he allowed me to partner her. She was shaking and semi-hysterical and her father was fuming, but he said nothing, and I could not play anymore, so we called it a day.

It seems that the regional chairman was well known for this. The talk was, never take your girlfriend or wife if she is attractive to a function where that regional chairman was present. One or two very ambitious young engineers were known to have hired a girlfriend for an event, allowing the chairman to 'take over' partway through the night.

I did not know anybody socially when I first arrived at the East Midlands plant and went to live in an apartment near the power plant. I joined the Intervarsity club in a nearby city, but they were not friendly to outsiders and any new member had to have a doctorate degree at least, so I joined an organization called The Coffee Pot and met my future wife there.

On honeymoon in Paris, I got an urgent call to go for interview at a power plant in Scotland. I offered to go, much to my wife's disgust. I could fly to Edinburgh and back the same day. The thrifty Scots would only pay the fare from my home address, so I told them to find someone else.

There was always an element of "hanky panky," as it was referred to, at the East Midlands plant. The management were allocated detached houses adjacent to the plant, and they paid a nominal rent of ten dollars a month. I was allocated one and lived in it the first three years of married life.

With the new management came a new hire, a beautiful secretary and known as 'Smelly Beryl' because she was perennially overloaded with perfume. Much to everyone's surprise and against normal convention, although single, she was allocated a four-bedroom detached house next the plant manager's house. The manager was often seen coming out of her house after midnight and a long 'working evening.'

For their services to the company, the plant manager and deputy were promoted to other stations, and a new plant manager and deputy manager took over.

All the time at this plant, there was never any threat of labor unrest, and everyone was quite happy to take on tasks that really were not in their normal duties. Everyone was given a nickname, most not exactly complimentary, but it was all part and parcel of a happy ship.

Having completed all my other courses, I was sent on a two-year MBA course involving a day off work and two evening classes a week. As part of the MBA, each year, I had to spend three weeks each, studying abroad in both Barcelona and Rotterdam, as well as management operations studies at a famous knitwear company near Nottingham—who gave me numerous samples to complement my wardrobe—and a small engineering company making oil burners in Ascot near London.

I was given the task of improving the oil supply and burners. With plant testing various coals as the station in future, we were going to have to change the hours to a two-shift operation (running only during the day and shutdown at night). The Newstead and Anaseley, Nottinghamshire coals were good coals, if a bit high in sulphur and chlorine (0.4%), but they had an unusual characteristic. The mineral matter in the coal, called ash, produced a completely transparent slag when heated in the furnace to melting point, just like glass. Normally, this would not have been a problem, except we had oil fired start-up burners in separate burner port holes. When the plant was operating at full load continuously, this was not an issue, but when the plant had to operate at lower loads or shutdown during the night and come on load early morning, this was a real problem. The glass-like slag put a barrier between the oil burners and the furnace, but the scanners could not see this barrier and started up the burners. The oil hit the glass-like slag and bounced straight back and set the area round the burner, outside the boiler, on fire. It took a lot of effort to examine and clean every burner (48 burners) every single night.

As I had a day a week studying from my MBA, this meant I had to accomplish everything in four days each week. A further complication was the management were all Freemasons and wanted me to ensure all their existing contracts with suppliers were maintained.

I was given a budget and a time to completion. I redesigned the whole oil burner system and produced my own coal/oil burner design which solved the problem within time and under budget (much to the disgust of the regional engineering development service who had their own Freemason contracting design company lined up to do the work).

All the personnel at the power plants were unionized with three unions, engineers, clerical staff, and manual workers. At this plant, as previously mentioned, unlike many other plants, the employees were docile and not prone to strike. One great advantage was the latest plant manager was surprisingly, a bit of a socialist and, even more strange, head of the engineering management union. This meant a relatively unified organization. During the miners' strike, the staff wanted to appear sympathetic to the miners' cause, but also to continue to operate as normal. The whole station staff were involved in subterfuge, and there was an air of excitement, all orchestrated by the plant manager. When it was known that the plant would be picketed, the manager organized a series of actions. Three large, rubber, low visibility "bowsers" (rubber storage vessels for liquids) were requisitioned from the army for storing light-up oil. Extra cylinders of hydrogen were also brought in. If we ran out of these items, they would be the most likely cause the station would have to shut down.

The main gate security building was made more comfortable with a fridge, freezer, cooker, and heating and beds installed in every room. At the same time, a camouflaged new route into the plant was built with movable trees blocking the approach. A month's supply of fuel was assembled, but also arrangements were made to bring in coal by truck (normally by rail) from non-unionized mines. The manager also recommended that all the station staff close their curtains at home when they had lights on to avoid advertising that they had power when some other parts of town possibly did not have power.

When the strike pickets arrived, they were welcomed with open arms. They were invited to place themselves in the main entrance security building with 'all mod cons' and erect a barrier across the main access road and the rail line, thereby 'blocking off' the plant. Photographs of them manning the barrier and in the entrance, building appeared on the national press with the heading, "Power plant completely shut-down!" Much to our amusement, the plant never missed a beat!

That manager was an absolutely great manager. He was later chairman of the Northern Ireland Electricity Company and known to this day as 'Jesus Christ' (his first initials were J.C.) for his actions in reducing the antagonism between Protestants and Catholics at power plants in Northern Ireland. Later still, he became chairman of the privatized Eastern Power Company and was knighted (Sir Jesus Christ?).

In England at that time, house prices were rocketing up. Even though we were paying only ten dollars a month in rent for the company-owned house, I could never save enough to match the rise in house prices. So, we bought a house from a couple who wanted to upsize and build a bigger new house and needed cash to start the project. We allowed the couple to continue to live in it, paying rent, for a year and then moved in. A year later, we sold the house for double what we paid for it!

When the next plant manager and deputy manager had once more moved on to higher positions, a decision was made by the new regional chairman to introduce 'pay and productivity' schemes to power plants, and to use our plant as the Guinea pig. The new management were enthusiastic but realized the whole management structure had to be changed. Up to then, I had only been responsible for three engineers and four office clerks, but under the new scheme, I was made responsible for what work and when maintenance activities were carried out, while the quality of work was the responsibility of the maintenance superintendent. All the foremen reported directly to me. To carry out this scheme, it was necessary to have written instructions for each task, and six clerks had to be employed to fill in the inputs for our new computer. I was allocated two long-time power plant employees and hired four others, all women.

One of the long-term employees and all four hired employees worked well, *but* the other long-term employee was a source of continuous problems. Apparently, she was well known as a troublemaker and was affectionately called 'Mrs. Bones.' She was not only habitually late for work but disturbed everyone else, always bringing her domestic problems to work. I tried everything: talking to her, referring her to human resources, as well as the station nurse even segregating her, and stationing her in my office. Often, she came into work in tears and dumped her personal problems on everyone, including me! It seems that she was having an affair with now one of *my* foremen. I was now responsible for both him and her, and he would not leave his wife for her. So double trouble!

I really did not want to or have the time to get involved, but all my efforts and efforts of many others to resolve this issue failed. They would not let me hand her back to her original department or sack her, saying once the pay and productivity system was up and running, she would have to come back to her original department anyway.

One day, she came in hysterical and uncontrollable. I told her to go and see the nurse and take the day off. The next day, she didn't turn up for work, so I called HR and they sent a person to see her. They found her slumped in her car, in her garage, with the engine left running. The police and ambulance were called, but she was pronounced dead at the scene.

That was bad enough, but almost as bad for the whole plant, she had left a really mind-boggling suicide note which said the foreman and been systematically stealing things from the power plant for years. She even revealed where these items were stored in a massive storage hut on a nearby farm.

All hell was let loose! There were not just small items like drills, grinders and other hand tools, bearings, and typical stores items, but also lathes, surface grinders, milling machines, radial drills and more, each weighing more than three tons. Nobody could understand how these items could not have been missed, or how they were gotten off site and through security. There was a court case, and I had to appear before the judge and jury as a witness for the prosecution. It is not fun being dragged in front of a court and seeing your every word distorted in the newspapers. The foreman got six years in jail, but all the staff at the power plant got blackballed (including me!) and further promotion for anyone was out of the question. They never found out who had assisted in stealing these items, but the mechanical maintenance engineer was demoted.

Could I have done more in the case of Mrs. Bones? I still ask that question of myself today!

Chapter 11: O, Canada!

A former person who had my job earlier had become Plymouth Power plant manager, but then fell out with the chairman and had left to join a small power company in Canada. In the meantime, the Quebec government nationalized the generating arm of this power company and set up their engineering company as a private consulting company with contracts from the Quebec government.

This former person invited me over to Canada to look over the engineering company with an idea to join it. I flew to Montreal and liked what I saw and decided there and then to join them.

From then on, it seems I was fated to be forever traveling!

My wife and I left the UK on August 2nd, 1974, and sailed on the Polish ship the MV Stefan Batory through the straits of Belle Isle, Newfoundland to Montreal. Approaching the Straits of Belle Isle, we could only travel in daylight, as we had to weave our way through the hundreds of icebergs at that time of year. The ship could not sail at night as icebergs can still not be seen by radar or acoustic sonar or any other modern devices—it seems that there has not been much improvement since the Titanic. It was eerie as at night, ice made a grinding sound as the waves bounced it against the hull of the stationary ship.

During the first week in Montreal, we went house hunting and found and signed up for an apartment. No sooner had we done this when I was told to catch a plane to Sydney, Cape Breton Island, Nova Scotia to go and solve energy problems at the steel plant there.

On entering the steelworks for the first time, my car was weighed and a permit to enter attached to the windscreen. Every time I left the plant, the car was weighed again. The blast furnaces contained solid copper cooling blocks weighing three hundred pounds each. It was not unknown for blocks to be stolen by securing them under a car.

I had never been in a steelworks before, let alone worked in one, but I quickly adapted. There was a large modernization program being implemented by a British company which had thrown up many energy problems, electricity, coal, oil, natural gas, coke oven gas, coke breeze, and blast furnace gas, so I set to work with great enthusiasm.

The first work was to convert the power boilers from burning oil to burn pulverized coal, coke oven gas, and blast furnace gas. As the blast furnace gas was very dirty, a venturi scrubber had to be designed and installed. Not so easy, as the gas was between 400 and 1,000 F entering the scrubber and only 150 F and saturated with water leaving it, as well as only 83 Btu/scf, which is a very low heating value.

Maybe I had too much enthusiasm, as two weeks later I was told that I was being assigned to the steelwork for a whole year to start with!

I wrote a letter to the management outlining my requirements. Their reaction was to accuse me of 'union tricks,' but in the end they gave me far better conditions and remuneration than I asked for, meaning I could easily run two houses, two cars, and so on, and live just off the allowances. What's more, I was allowed at least two all-paid business trips a year *back* to the UK!

Emigrating from the U.K.? I was back in the U.K. eight weeks after arriving in Canada. Sydney via Gander Newfoundland was only a four-hour flight to Prestwick airport, Glasgow!

We rented the ground floor apartment of a house in Sydney. It turned out the second floor was occupied, and the house owned by a well-known 'Madam' who serviced the mayor and corporation of the city. I was really welcomed into a team of British, Canadian and South African engineers. Except for the weather in mid-winter (blinding snowstorms with drifts nine feet deep and having to walk backwards to work as it was impassable for cars), it was like being in the U.K.! One advantage of being there was I could get hold of tickets to all the upcoming events at the following year's Montreal Olympic Games. I used some and sold the most prestigious tickets at a handsome profit.

I was invited to become a 1st Lieutenant in the 2nd Battalion, Nova Scotia Highlanders Regiment. Most of the managers at the steel plant were senior officers in the national guard type regiment. I was allowed to do this even with a British passport, as I had not been commissioned (or even been any other rank) in the British army. Apparently being a P. Eng. (Profession Engineer of Nova Scotia) allowed me to be commissioned. I even played in the regiment's pipe band when they were short of pipers.

Our original idea was to spend Christmas and New Year in Nova Scotia, but it transpired that all the British engineers were heading home for the holidays and the work would likely come to a standstill, so we joined the group going back to the U.K.

My wife left ten days before Christmas, and I booked a flight three days before Christmas. My wife arranged to stay with her mother, who was a matron at an Old people's home who had gotten off work. The evening after my wife left, I got home from work in Sydney and switched of the TV to hear breaking news that an old people's home had caught fire in England, and there were fatalities. It was the very same old people's home my mother-in-law was matron of!

It was 6 pm in Nova Scotia and 10 pm in England. I tried to phone but could not get through. It seems after travelling all night, my wife and her mother decided to go to bed early, but were awakened by the police to get them to return to the old people's Most of that Christmas was spent with the police and various other services trying to find out what had happened. Six people died and five more were badly burned. A court of enquiry later concluded that one old dear had disabled the fire alarm in her room and fell asleep smoking in bed. Due to a strong wind and the design of the false ceiling with no fire breaks, a whole wing of the building caught fire rapidly, and no blame was attached to my mother-in-law.

One of the managers decided to take my wife and I to a 'famous' restaurant located at the Louisbourg fortress (built in 1740 by the French and their major location in North America). The manager politely asked the waitress what she would recommend on the menu, and he was absolutely floored when the waitress said, "Oh, I wouldn't eat any of it!"

The main dish in Cape Breton was lobster washed down with dark navy rum. The people at work were not averse to downing four or five lobsters and a bottle of rum over an evening.

At the end of the year in Sydney, they tried to pressure me to stay in Nova Scotia, but I insisted on going back to Montreal and we bought a house there. WRONG! The Quebecois government, six months later, brought in a law to say all engineering work carried out in Quebec had to done in French, and the company sent me to study French, which I was relatively wooden at.

The house we bought was in the English Ghetto, as the French Canadians called it. Eighty percent of the French Canadian's were friendly. Ten percent were ambivalent, but ten percent were openly verbally hostile: being called a *Tabernac* was the normal insult used, rude to them, worse than the F word.

We had arranged a holiday to Cuba over Christmas when I was called into the company's chief engineer's office. "Would I be willing to work in Cuba and assist not only the Canadian government, but also the U.S. government?" At that time there was a *rapprochement* between the Cuban government and the U.S. government, but still, U.S. citizens could not go to or work in Cuba at that time. I agreed, provided I got written authorization from all three governments. With great fanfare, and four massive chests of luggage, we set off from Montreal on the flight to Cuba and were met with a Cuban government delegation. We were treated like royalty, and I was awarded the Order of Lenin after the work was completed! The Order of Lenin is a very high prestigious award in Communist countries, so I don't think it was real.

In between all of this, my eldest daughter was born in Montreal.

I was sent on a Canadian government emergency rescue team to Guyana (previously British Guyana) where the farmers had burnt the sugar cane crops which in turn caused the overhead transmission line to melt from the Garden of Eden power plant into Georgetown, the Capital. My task was to get the old Kingston Power Plant in Georgetown up and running again, which by then was being used as a laundry.

At that time, there was a major political problem. Some sixty percent of the population were Asian from India, brought in by the British colonial administration to run the civil service, water, power and sewage facilities. Thirty-five percent were of African origin, originally, brought in as slaves and then as manual workers starting in the eighteen-hundreds, and even though the population is predominantly of Asian origin, the government was really a dictatorship as all higher officials are of African origin and

Communist. Everyone had to be called comrade. I worked under the direct instruction of the Comrade Minister of Energy, Jack.

There was great animosity between the African majority and the Asian minority. The Africans were relatively poor, but the Asians displayed affluence which I found to be not in their interests. The government put server restrictions on the Asian population who wanted to get out of the country by any means possible. Asian women would try anything, and I mean anything, to get out, including offering gold and sex.

For entertainment there was the hotel swimming pool and the cinema. The infamous Pegasus Hotel (called Peg-arse-us by my first girlfriend's husband, who also stayed there) had a swimming pool with old-fashioned deck chairs. It was really the iron curtain. On the left side the shallow end was the Canadian contingent, in the middle the American contingent, and at the deep end, the British contingent. On the right side the shallow end was reserved for the Guineans, but there was never anybody there. In the middle were the Russians and, at the deep end, the East Germans. The Westies kept to the left-hand side of the pool and the Communists to the right-hand side.

The cinema was showing the classic British comedies in the 'Carry On' series which always have sexual innuendos. On the fourth night I was there, I tried to buy a ticket, but was sold out. On the next night, 'Carry on Camping,' I managed to buy one of the last tickets. The cinema was packed; it was more like a football crowd than a cinema. Laughing, screaming, jumping up standing up cheering, stamping their feet, and roaring. I had difficult imagining that the audience could understand the double meaning from most of the conversation.

At work, all the major countries were offering their services. Gas turbines arrived from Canada, USA, U.K., East Germany, and Russia. These were all useless, as there was no gas supply, and the only available fuel oil was from Cuba and Venezuela and was contaminated, perhaps intentionally, with seawater. I found two small old lubricating oil centrifuges to remove the seawater from the fuel oil and got the power plant working about twenty percent of capacity, as that was the limit of the centrifuges. I tried to get Comrade Minister Jack to import more centrifuges and or buy fuel oil from different sources, but he would not listen. I was glad to leave once I had got it up and running even at twenty percent capacity.

A steam pipe burst in the power plant of a paper mill in Cornerbrook, Newfoundland, and I was sent to affect a temporary repair. It was the middle of winter, but I was able to fly into Stephenville and drive in a hire car to Cornerbrook. I worked for twenty-four hours solid in the cold, damp, and smelly conditions and managed to fix a temporary repair and suggest a more permanent repair one new parts arrived from Boston. The weather closed in, and I was stranded, but it warmed up for two days to just about freezing. At the end of two days, I decided to make a break for it with two others from the plant.

We fitted chains to the hired car tires and bought shovels and set off to Deer Lake, forty miles away, which we believed still had planes flying in and out, while Stephenville was completely snowed in. We would drive for half a mile and then hit a deep snow drift. We all took turns to dig. The first drift took an hour to dig through and the second, another mile ahead, another hour. The third drift, two miles beyond that, was relatively small, so it only took half an hour, but the fourth drift was very big and kept filling as we moved the snow. We kept using the car as a battering ram and finally after two more hours digging, we were through and there were no more drifts. We were absolutely exhausted, but luckily, we arrived just in time to drop the car off and catch the plane. Back in Montreal, I went down with pneumonia and was off work for three weeks.

The Canadian government decided to carry out a massive study into Fundy Tidal Power. The Bay of Fundy as one of the highest tidal surges in the world with the tide difference being more the fifty feet. The idea was to build a barrage with some 4,000 MWe of hydro turbines, making it the largest hydro project in the world at that time. All the consulting engineering companies were involved, and my area was 'tidal fill.' It was a very interesting green energy concept.

One of the major issues was that the tide could only generate for a maximum of twelve hours per day, generating on the incoming and outgoing tide twice per day. This meant 4,000 MWe of power was required the other twelve hours per day. Some other hydro projects could fill in part of this, but nuclear plants were out of the question due to not being able to cycle on and off or high-load and low-load. Only thermal power plants, simple cycle gas turbines, or specially designed coal fired units could do this. I got the job of looking at how thermal power plants could fill the gap. I visited all the power plants in New Brunswick, Nova Scotia, and even Maine and New Hampshire. I worked with designers to look at building a 200 MWe self-supporting wood-burning Biomass power plant in New Brunswick, which would operate twelve hours each day. We also investigated building new coal fired units with fast start-up turbines at both Grand Lake, New Brunswick and Halifax, Nova Scotia. The study was completed but the cost was astronomic, and the idea was quickly dropped. They did build a small test tidal scheme at Digby on the Fundy, and that is still in operation today.

There were numerous other crackpot schemes, one to generate hydro power in Labrador, which has massive potential for hydro power but no industry to use it. The idea was to dig a tunnel under the Straits of Belle Isle and supply power to Newfoundland. Due to the icebergs which bottomed out and ground down the floor of the strait, it was not possible to lay an undersea cable. The idea died, as building a twenty-mile tunnel was ultra-expensive.

Chapter 12:
Relocation to Germany

Returning to work in Montreal, I found the company had been bought out by a large German power company. Within a month I was posted to Essen, Germany to work on the new, massive at that time, 750 MWe units being designed and built. Nobody there spoke English, but I had no difficulty working in German or conversing with their staff. However, I was not welcomed by the boiler department manager at my new post. He told me, "I was never consulted; I have no idea what to do with you!" He gave me an office, a secretary, and tons of documents to read, all of which were in German, as well as invitations to tender and tender documents from every supplier of everything bought by the company. I was told to make recommendations of which items to buy, knowing full well they had already decided. I soon realized my secretary's job was to restrict my access to anyone else in the company. At the end of the week, I reported this back to my new German manager who was now based in Montreal. His reply was, "Oh, no problem, just tell the secretary to go out and buy three bottles of schnapps, three bottles of champagne, three bottles of cognac and twenty bottles of beer as well as schnapps glasses and beer glasses and send the bill to me. Get the secretary to put the drinks and glasses on your desk."

Everyone in the company saw her staggering back carrying all the booze, and as soon as the secretary left my office, there was a knock on my office door. "My name is xxx and I would like to welcome you to the company.

I replied, "Oh, pleased to meet you. Come in, would you like a drink?"

Within ten minutes, my office was full of people, and fifteen minutes later the German manager appeared at the door laughing and holding his hands up saying, "I am beaten!"

Everything went well after that. There were frequent drinking parties in the office in working time, and they operated indefinite flextime where you were required to put in 150 hours a month with four weeks' vacation and a vacation bonus. Most people worked ten hours or more a day at the start of the month and never appeared at work most of the last week of the month. I got a living allowance of 150 deutsche marks a day, which was more than enough for us to live on.

My wife and I, along with our two-year-old daughter, rented an apartment in Bredeney opposite the Krupp mansion, Villa Hugel. It was okay to start with, but as it got colder in late autumn, there was an issue. The owners only turned the heating on during the evening and never started it up again until 4 pm. When we complained, they said all the other tenants of the apartments were at work during the day and they would not put it on just for my wife and daughter. Fortunately, we found a lady who was happy for us to share her large apartment and play with our two-year-old daughter. Six months there and our daughter was speaking German with a strong local accent, saying for instance "Yo," instead of *Ja* for yes.

* * *

At the end of the first year, I was asked to go and work in Erlangen, Bavaria to be an intermediary between the Iranian government's agent, the UK power company I used to work for, and Siemens, who were building the Bushehr nuclear power plant in Iran. As well as my expense allowance for being in Essen, I was also given another 100 deutsche marks a day living allowance being for assigned from Essen to Erlangen. I was now getting 250 deutsche marks a day, equivalent to $500 today, plus my normal salary. I could live like a lord.

We moved from Essen to Erlangen in Bavaria and rented an upstairs apartment in the affluent sector from the retired medical doctor of Siemens. His family were very good with all of us and frequently invited us to drink champagne with them. People at work invited us for coffee, but their phrasing was very strange. "We would like you to come to us for coffee… would three weeks on Wednesday be convenient?" Talk about planning in advance!

I nearly got fired on my first day. My part of the open plan office had only a broken-down chair. As the next office section was not used, I changed my chair for one in the next section. The next day I was charged with illegally entering the next section to obtain sensitive secret documentation and threated with the sack. My boss in Essen stepped in and told them not to be so stupid.

All the documentation and instructions for building and operating the nuclear power plant in Iran had to be in English, but approved and signed off by the German TUV standards institute. It was crazy; I don't know who translated the German into English or who was the TUV official who stamped the translation, but they were full of intentional wrong statements, and once stamped they could not be changed or corrected. For instance, a correct translation of the German should have said, "This sheet has four parts." The English TUV approved, translation said, "This shit has four farts." And this is for a NUCLEAR Power Plant!

My section head had an apartment in Munich. For two weeks when my wife and daughter went to England to visit her mother, it was Oktoberfest. My section head gave me the keys to his apartment, and I went to Munich for a long weekend. I am not a big beer drinker, as I prefer red wine, but I decided to go. The whole long weekend was torrential rain and nearly everyone was soaked to the skin. The worst were many English, Irish, and Dutch young people who were camping. They said their campsite was completely flooded out, and all their gear wet through. They all sat there, with nowhere else to go, wet through, not happy campers. The um-papa bands tried their best to raise everyone spirits, but everyone was like damp squibs, and I was happy to leave after just two nights there.

After three months in Erlangen and on a trip back to Montreal, I complained about the inaccuracies in the translation, but to no avail. In the office on Dorchester Boulevard (now Boulevard Rene Leveque), I suddenly got a phone call. The voice said, "Where are you, you should be here?"

I said, "I am here, who are you?"

The voice said, "I am from a large oil company, and you have an interview with me right now at the Queen Elizabeth Hotel." I knew the place, as it just down the Boulevard from our office in Montreal. I expressed surprise, as I knew nothing about an interview, but agreed to walk down the street and meet him. He explained he was head hunting me to take charge of the power and utility plant for a major oil sands development in Alberta, and was I interested? He laid out the work and the terms: 50% more than I was getting, with a $100,000 interest free loan to buy a house in Calgary. I would be always based in Calgary, work a 35-hour week, and have every third Friday off. It all sounded interesting, I left saying, "Send me a written offer and I will consider it."

Four months later when I was back in Germany, I got a letter via numerous different addresses offering me the job and saying, "Please reply by September 1st ..." it was then December 2nd! I phoned them explaining I had only just got the letter to which he replied, "Are you still interested?"

I immediately said, "Yes, and the earliest I could start is February 1st," which he agreed to.

I resigned from the consulting company but had to work the rest of December in Germany then move back to Montreal, sell the house, and move to Calgary in mid-winter by February 1st. Moving three times in a month, in the middle of winter, Germany, Montreal and Calgary was a mammoth struggle.

The Germans tried to insist on me working to the end of February, but something happen which meant that the whole project fell through, and I was very lucky to leave when I did. The Shah of Iran was deposed in January, and the revolutionary guards took over and smashed all the equipment for the almost finished reactor. Suddenly the whole project team of two thousand engineers and other staff were out of a job! My timing was perfect!

Chapter 13: The Oil Company

During my first week at the major oil company, they had a 'Bull Session.' A bull session is held in a main hotel for the whole project staff with food and drink, followed by a question-and-answer session by management. Having the food and drink first meant most people were well-oiled before the question-and-answer session.

The very first question was the last! A big guy, West Point graduate, from the oil company's headquarters in New York got up and in a semi-drunken state said, "What I want to know is, why are all the management dwarfs round here?" They were actually all short as were their PAs. Immediately, the PAs rushed at the guy and started a fist fight! The whole place was bedlam, and it was decided to end the session early with no more questions. They continued to have Bull Sessions, but from then on had the question-and-answer session *before* the food and drink!

Such was my introduction to the oil business.

My car was shipped to Montreal, then to Calgary, and I picked it up at the railway goods yard. The gas/petrol line immediately froze as it was -10 F in Calgary. My first girlfriend, who now lived in Calgary with her family, arranged a realtor, and we bought a house.

This house had a fantastic view from the picture window of our living room across the Sarcee Indian Reservation, which is now the Tsuut'ina 145 First Nation, and which included the peaks of the Rocky Mountains. All our greater family came to visit, and we spent a great first summer in the mountains barbecuing with new and old friends alike. In fact, every summer was great. My friends from Germany came, and we toured Alberta and British Colombia in a hired twenty-seven-foot motorhome.

We had no sooner moved into the house in Calgary when my manager appeared at the door. A manager coming to the house? I knew immediately there was something wrong. He said, "A decision had been made to move my part of the project to New York and would I move to New York?"

I said, "No way!" We had moved enough in the last six weeks. He reluctantly agreed they had promised I would not be moved out of Calgary, and they would allow me to work on it in Calgary and make trips to New York.

We really enjoyed Calgary. Except for the brutal winters, it was the best place to live in the whole world. Our second daughter was born in Calgary. The people there are terrific, friendly, smiling, and always had a good word even for complete strangers. Everybody at work were friends, except a couple of managers who never even said one word to each other in two years. One floor of our office building was an indoor gymnasium with an oval running track, badminton court, squash courts, and every type of fitness training machine with team building fitness programs in working hours, especially in winter. Another floor had three complete restaurants for the employees only. There was no division of sexes, not even when camping on team development trips.

My first trip outside of Canada for the oil company was to a conference and exhibition at the Astrodome, Houston. There was nothing exceptional on the trip, but on the return Air Canada flight leaving Houston with a short stop in Denver, I was bumped up to first class. I sat back and made myself comfortable, removed my jacket and put my computer bag with my documentation in it, in the overhead locker as well as my cabin baggage. Fifteen minutes after arriving in Denver, a message came out of the loudspeaker system saying, "Will Mr. Nib please report to gate 33 desk?" I asked the cabin staff what gate were we at, and is it me they want and why? I was told, "Yes, it is you they want, and we are at gate 33 and there is a message for you, so just leave your things onboard and go up the jet way"

I got to the desk, and they said, "You are bumped off the flight."

WHAT? I know people can get bumped off a flight, but I never realized you can be bumped off in *middle* of a flight!

I told them, "I have only my wallet with me. My ticket, boarding card, passport, and driving license are in my computer bag, so I cannot leave the plane at least until I get my luggage."

They replied, "Oh don't worry, everything will be waiting for you in Calgary when you get there *tomorrow*, and in the meantime, we will put you up in a nearby hotel as the plane is about to take off."

I said, "Call the police or I will call the police and take whatever action is necessary to stop that flight leaving. You cannot take my passport off me and leave me stranded in the USA without identity."

Without waiting, I picked up their phone and dialed 911 Panic!

I do not know what the police said, but the airline staff tried to argue with them. A few minutes later, a US immigration official arrived and stated that the airline was able to bump me off the plane but were not entitled to remove my passport and documentation and declared, "The plane cannot leave until at least his documents are returned to him."

Following a conference, it was agreed they would collect my jacket and computer bag from the plane, but not my hand luggage. It was not fun being taken to a hotel in Denver in November when it was 28 F, and I had no coat or PJs. Finally, they put me on an early morning flight the next day and I was reunited with my baggage.

The third winter in Calgary, the weather was especially bad, with temperatures down to -30 F. That winter, the weather was also bad back in the UK and my father got stranded in deep snow at 15 F, got frostbite and ended up in hospital with gangrene in his foot. A decision was made to amputate his leg. The company arranged meetings in New York for me at short notice and, within six hours of hearing about my father, I was on a plane to New York and on to

Gatwick Airport, London. The idea after arriving at Gatwick at 6 am was a plane to Manchester and car to the hospital in Blackburn.

At Gatwick, it was 15 F, and the flight to Manchester had been cancelled as well as the trains into London or anywhere else. Searching round, I found a small regional airline with a flight to Liverpool and managed to get a seat. We circled round Liverpool airport, but it was covered in freezing fog. Running short on fuel, we landed at Chester Racecourse which had a small landing strip, and we were unceremoniously dumped out of the plane on the racecourse in deep snow, some 20 miles from Liverpool.

How to get the 60 miles to Blackburn when everything seemed to be snowed in? I walked through the snow to the bus station and found a local bus still operating the 18 miles to Warrington. I think it stopped at every small village on the way. I then found a bus to Preston via Wigan, and then a bus to Blackburn, getting to the hospital five hours *after* the operation. My first girlfriend's parents met me and took me and my mother every day for a week to visit him. At the end of the week, he seemed to be improving and I had to be back in New York for the concocted meeting. I left him singing "How Great Thou Art" with the Salvation Army band playing during their visit to the hospital. Sad to say, he died two weeks later.

The project was advancing well, but the Alberta energy resources conservation board mandated that the whole project was coal-fired, which was not technically possible—a long other story. Our team had already developed a strategy where the main fuel for 'Huff and Puff'

injection steam production was natural gas. I developed a strategy using coal as the utility fuel. The senior management wanted coal completely out of the equation, so they were not too thrilled that I had proposed a solution which would achieve the oil company's requirements and the Alberta energy board's requirements but, in the end, that strategy was adopted as the basis.

Our team did a tour of Europe to visit coal-fired plants in Germany, the U.K., and Denmark. We arrived in Dusseldorf, Germany four days before Carnival Rosenmontag (the day before Shrove Tuesday-Mardi Gras) and had a whale of a time celebrating. On Ash Wednesday, we flew to Manchester, U.K. and visited my old power plants. We even took a detour for tea with my mother in Accrington before flying on to Denmark. Another wild time commenced in Copenhagen. Even the Canadians were not used to being served beer with lunch at plant canteens.

It did not last. We worked on that basis for two years and were in the process of awarding major contracts when the company pulled the plug on the whole project. I, and most others, were out of a job!

The oil company came up with a proposition. They "asked" me to join the coal and minerals division, which was involved in developing two coal mines in Canada and help headquarters in New York on the construction of a major power plant in Hong Kong. My job was to assess the power plant market internationally to take the coal from the company mines. I agreed to this. In mid-June, 1982, I began my life with the coal and minerals company.

Chapter 14:
Coal and Minerals in Canada

I had not been involved in the decision to buy and develop the coal mines. The coal quality from the mines were 'difficult' (an understatement). A German power company later stated, "The coal is only fit for fire extinguishers!" It was a major challenge to get power companies to buy the coal, and even more difficult to get the plant operators to burn it successfully.

The problem was, the coal had been laid down before mountain building, and had been moved, ground, devolatilized, and rolled into a ball some twenty miles from where it had been laid down. The miners liked it, as the seam was 120 feet thick and easy to mine with a good heating value and very low sulphur. It was called 'Coal Berg' locally.

It was difficult with this coal to keep a stable flame, due to low volatility, in a typical power plant boiler and turned to dust on handling, but that was of little interest to the miners. The miners made it known that it was my job to get it to burn! To make matters worse, the Canadian government's energy board issued a report at that time to say the coal was un-usable.

The CEO of the coal and minerals company was an exceptionally flamboyant character called Dr. James Green. He was the one instrumental in buying the coal mines, and in his eyes, it was success at any cost. He looked at the economics and said it was a money-maker, with no idea about the limitations of the coal for use in the power industry.

He frequently got in trouble with police. One example was driving his new sports car after a meeting at the mine on a long stretch of straight road doing 100 mph, but suddenly slowing down before a police radar stop. They searched his car and found a secret radar detector. He got fined, lost his license for six months, and the equipment was ripped out of his car. He also presented his business card to a far east CEO with a condom attached.

I wrote a paper trying to direct the use of the coals towards the cement industry, to which the CEO agreed, but only as an addition to the power industry. He signed contracts with an Ontario power company who were desperate for coal at the time. In 1974, Richard Nixon had mandated that no USA fuel could be sold outside the USA, and that mandate was still in effect. They ignored all the negative quality implications, figuring that they could be solved later, and took one of the big four Japanese companies and the largest Korean company as agents. I was the only technical person involved in determining how and where our coal could be used. All the other managers were marketing types. Despite their different backgrounds, they were all great guys, and they all supported one another and were open to new ideas.

At this point, the travelling really started.

My first trip outside Canada in support of these mines was to a cement company in Oahu, Hawaii. The cement plant was tucked away between two mountains on the northwest corner of Oahu where tourists did not venture. I was told not to hang around that part of Oahu as the coast was full of hobos, druggies, drunks, and people sleeping rough. Inland were hostile Oahu natives who associated any white person in the area as being a hobo. It was not your typical Hawaiian scene.

The cement plant was run by an ex-US navy commander who ran the plant like they were still on a ship. We always had to address the manager as "commander." Fortunately, the test went well without problems, and I was actually glad to get away from the area.

The next trip, three weeks later, was a big trip to Malaysia, Hong Kong, and Korea, my first ever visit to these countries. In Malaysia, the meeting went well and founded the groundwork for future cooperation with the power company. In the evening after the meeting, we had dinner at the former British commissioner's residence. I do not know what I ate, but I was violently sick later that evening. The following morning, I had to drag myself onto the plane for Hong Kong and just about managed to keep going during the meeting in Hong Kong the next day. Once again, we drew up a plan for testing the coal in the plant soon to be commissioned. I was in a bad way, fighting to keep going and could not eat. Immediately after the meeting, I went to bed.

The next morning saw me on another plane to Korea. I went to a meeting there and straight to bed without food. The following morning, I was taken by car right across Korea from Seoul to the Samchok Cement Plant. I was starting to feel better until I smelt kimchi; I can't stand the stuff or the smell of the stuff. I somehow survived and had two days rest at the weekend in Seoul before flying back to Vancouver and onto Calgary. It took me two weeks to fully recover!

The next trip, some three weeks after I recovered from the stomach problems, I went to Japan. Our hosts, the major Japanese trading company, invited us to their 'nest' and I was allocated a Japanese girl to show me round for the next two days, which was a weekend. At the nest, I made a major *faux pas*. I was offered a glass of the company's forty-year-old stock of the finest single-malt Whiskey, which went for at least $600 a bottle. Much to everyone's horror, I declined and asked for cognac! A big loss of face! The trip had mixed results after that.

A month later it was back to Korea with much fanfare for the signing of a contract with the Korean power company. Our CEO and marketing manager were in attendance. Following the contract signing the next day, there was to be an evening celebratory Kee Sing Party. The evening we arrived; I went to the bar. Sitting next to me was a Belgium guy who asked me what I was doing. He told me to be very careful at a *Kee Sing Party*, as it was all set up to embarrass the guests and have a psychological hold over you. The hosts would provide all the people at the party with very high-class girls whose job it was to fulfil all our needs. We were not supposed to do anything. The girls would give us drinks, would feed us, would take our trousers down and hold onto our penises when we went to the toilet, and clean us up and take you back to their 'nests' after the meal.

The Belgian said, "Watch very carefully. The host's girl will drink most of a glass and hand the almost empty glass to the host, while your girl will take a sip and make you drink almost all the glass. Be ready to be stripped naked in front of everyone and even be sexually assaulted. The Korean theory is that you can only have a working relationship if you get rid of all your inhibitions. They are happier for you to get rid of your inhibitions than for the Koreans to get rid of theirs." The Belgian further said there is only one way to get out of it: "Vomit!" He gave me some tablets which he said would make me instantly throw up without any aftereffects.

The Kee Sing Party got going, exactly as the Belgian guy had said. When it was still reasonably respectable, although our CEO was already 'getting to know' his girl, our marketing manager asked the host CEO if he had any family.

He replied, "Yes, a son and daughter."

The marketing manager said, "Oh good, I have two daughters myself. What do your children do?"

Their CEO frowned uncomfortably and said, "My son is doing a Ph.D. at university."

Our marketing manager went on and then asked, "What does your daughter do?"

There was an even bigger frown, more squirming in his seat and a reluctance to answer. When pressed further, he said, "What my daughter does is her affair. Her job is to fund my son's education. You can ask her yourself! She is getting to know your CEO at the other side of the table right at this moment."

I took a tablet and left the party in full swing!

The following morning, we assembled for a meeting, and after half an hour, in walked the girls from the Kee Sing Party. The host apparently asked the girls how everyone had performed during the night. It seems that our CEO did not just take his girl, the CEO's daughter, to bed, but also my girl as well. They gave a lurid description of his performance to great applause. Naturally the hosts' actions were never discussed.

I came to the idea that in Japan, they would never try to embarrass you, whereas in Korea, they would *definitely* try to embarrass you. Our CEO, however, was beyond embarrassment.

✳ ✳ ✳

Finally realizing the coal from the mines was a hard sell, the CEO considered blending the coal with other coals and hired an eminent professor to see if he could come up with a 'beneficiation solution.' He hired a professor, Blue Jones from the University of Melbourne, Australia. Blue was as much a character as the CEO, and they had frequent clashes. The CEO liked to wear white suites to meetings, and it was typical of Blue to say, "Good morning, Colonel Sanders!" to the CEO. The breaking point came when Blue proposed grinding up the coal, froth floating it, and briquetting it. The idea was sound, but completely uneconomic.

Blue had already briquetted some samples in the form of, and he called them 'ice hockey pucks.' Blue said the pucks were strong enough not to break down in handling and could maintain flame stability due to adding an oil-based binder. I am sure that was correct. We were on the 22nd floor in the glass-walled conference room, and he proceeded to show how stable they were by throwing one at a window. The window shattered and rained glass down on 4th Avenue sidewalk. Fortunately, only one person was on that part of the sidewalk at that the time and wasn't seriously injured. Blue was instantly sacked, and that was the end of 'beneficiation.'

The next trip, a few weeks later, was to Kaohsiung, Taiwan where we had signed a contract with a cement company. I was there at the quay side to meet the ship, and what a sight! The ship had been caught in a typhoon and the bow was stove in, the hatch covers half-off, and the ship's holds were full of sea water. They just continued as though nothing was wrong. The coal was grabbed out of the ship and dumped in trucks. Black sludge poured from the grabs and from the trucks which took the coal through the center of Kaohsiung to the plant. We did not need to find our way to the plant. There was a two-inch-deep track of black coal sludge all the way from the quay thorough the city center to the plant. As it took four days to unload the ship, the sludge got thicker and thicker and covered not only the whole road but also the footpaths and adjacent streets. In the mornings, women came out of their shops doing yoga exercise, knee deep in black sludge. I felt very embarrassed, but nobody complained, and nobody did anything to clear up the mess.

Back at the ship, I was told the next cargo for the ship was *sugar*, and painters arrived to paint the holds white with the holds still half full of coal. Undeterred, they started painting while the grabs were still digging out the wet sludge. What a mess, I couldn't look! Coal dust mixed with the white paint. I hid away at the cement plant and left as soon as possible.

Finally, I visited the plant in Hong Kong, where our company was the majority shareholder. Soon after start-up, it was arranged to send a test parcel of our coal in the same ship as a test parcel from another mine.

At 1 am, in Calgary, I was awoken by a telephone call from Hong Kong to say get here immediately, as the ship was going to dock in the next twelve hours. As it took at least twenty-four hours to get from home to the plant, I rushed round like crazy and got to the plant thirty-six hours after the telephone call. The ship had arrived, but inadvertently they started unloading the other coal first and then said it would be a *week* before they started unloading our coal.

What to do? There was no point in flying back to Calgary, as the round trip would have taken three days at least with no rest. There were no sleeper seats in business class in those days! My CEO said, "Oh, just stay there, or go up to China and have a good time!"

It took a couple of days to get a visa and find a tour going to remote spots. I met a German girl on the trip, and we agreed to watch one another's backs. We were taken to a big store which had no customers in it. It was dirty, too. On the counters were all sorts of furs. Mink, arctic fox, rabbit, and many others I had never heard off. They were very cheap, but I was deeply suspicious.

Back in Hong Kong, we met a Canadian furrier by accident and related our story. He asked where we had been and why we had not bought the furs at such a cheap price. We had no expertise in furs and questioned whether the furs were mink or Arctic Fox at all. The furrier said, "I know where you have been, and those are genuine mink and arctic fox. The only problem is they are not cured correctly and are poorly cut and sewn together. What you *should* have done is bought two coats, brought them back to Hong Kong or Canada, had them cut up, then cured, then re-sewn together, and then you would have had a Mink or Arctic Fox coat for a quarter of the price in the stores in Hong Kong or Canada." You live and learn!

I stayed in Hong Kong Sheraton Hotel, Kowloon side. The group that went to China met again at Ned Kelley's Last Stand, a bar with a jazz band in Kowloon, which was great fun. During that trip, I was allowed to spend one night at the Peninsula Hotel, the most splendid hotel in Hong Kong, just to say that I'd stayed there. We also visited Tai O, on Lantau Island, which was still a small, isolated fishing village at that time.

The large power plant my company had the majority stake was located at the base of Castle Peak, a mountain on the mainland New Territories of Kowloon in an unpopulated rocky slope into the Pearl River estuary. It was made from two small rocky islands, and the cliff blasted to fill in with rock. The English name on the plant was Castle Peak, but the Chinese name is *Tap Shek Kok* (meaning steppingstones) *Fat Teen Chong* (power station). This caused a lot of confusion as the taxi drivers would take you up the mountain if you asked for Castle Peak.

The nearest small village was *Tuen Moon*, which was at that time a Haka village but is now a large town. The hotels were either on Hong Kong Island or in *Tsim Sha Tsui*, Kowloon and the company associated hotels were there. In the early 1980s, travelling from the hotels to the power plant was not simple. First you had to walk to the star ferry and catch a ferry to Hong Kong Island. Then you had to walk to a small jetty where the hovercraft took you to Tuen Moon. This was usually a rough ride, as the hovercraft had to dodge round the many ships and their wake produced large waves that at sometimes, brought the hovercraft to a violent stop. At *Teun Moon* there was a rudimentary jetty and walkway. Taxi drivers at that time were not too thrilled at taking you to the power plant as the road was filled with construction traffic and the road in poor condition. Thus, it took at least one and a half hour each way to the power plant. Ferries only ran during the day, so at night you could only get to and from the plant at shift change when a bus ran the two-hour road journey to *Tim Sha Tsui*.

It turned out that the first cargo to Hong Kong of our coal was oxidized. Oxidized coal normally is easier to burn but the heating value is lower. This shipment performed much better than the typical coal from the mine. I had to work both day and some nights, as they insisted we test at low loads which could only be at night. The daytime tests at full load were great and better than I could have expected. I thought the nighttime tests went well, too, but the operators were not convinced and wanted a *second* test! *<Sigh>*. Test cargoes were priced lower than contract cargoes, so it was in the power company's interest to request more tests.

In the meantime, they had sold a shipment to a Philippine nickel plant, subject to successful testing. The nickel plant was owned by a Canadian company and was located on a remote island called Nonoc, between Leyte and Mindanao. The area is famous, as during the second World War the Japanese fleet had been sunk in the Surigao Channel off Nonoc.

I was given enough notice this time and set off the shortest route: Calgary-Hawaii-Guam-Manila-Cebu-Nonoc. What a joke to consider that route short! I had to stay over in Manila one night. Arriving at the airport at 8 pm, I went outside to get a taxi. At that time, it was relatively quiet with no taxis in sight, so I put my two bags down on the ground at the taxi rank. Instantly, two young men who had been lurking in the dark under cover behind me rushed forward, each grabbing one bag and rushed off shouting, "Taxi, taxi!"

I gave chase, but I had just come off a ten-hour flight and was not up to speed. I followed them off the concourse to a beat-up car just as they were putting my bags in the trunk. I asked them to remove my bags, but they tried to assure me they were a taxi. By then there were three of them! What to do? Finally, I asked, "Can you take me to the Intercontinental Hotel?"

They said "Yes," so off we went. Within minutes, I noticed we were not going in the direction of Manila but the other way. I told them to stop the car but said, "Oh, don't worry, we need gas."

We pulled up at a gas station and they said, "We have no money for gas." Again, it was a tricky situation. The gas station had no phone, so I just risked it and paid for the gas. I was sweating on the top line, but fortunately for me, they did take me to the hotel. By then I was tired and hungry, so I dumped my luggage in my room and went down to the restaurant for something to eat. Feeling full and after a glass of wine I staggered back to my room, only to find a young lady in my bed. I really did kick her out.

It was the monsoon season but the flight the next day to Cebu was okay. The onward flight to Nonoc from Cebu in a four-seater plane though thunderstorms and continuous rain was very bumpy, and we were bounced around the whole flight. I was picked up at the airport and was taken to a straw thatched hut with a veranda. I had only been in the hut two hours when there was a knock on the door, and there was a beautiful young lady, and I mean *beautiful*, who said, "I am your temporary wife; I am here to give you every comfort, food, drink, cleaning, and sex at your pleasure!"

"Oh, for god's sake!" I cried. "But I would like some dinner and a glass of wine!" The bed was very uncomfortable, too soft for my liking, and I ended up trying to sleep on the floor, but the incessant rain on the tin veranda roof sounded like a continuous drum roll and sleeping was impossible.

Thank goodness I didn't get there earlier! The day before I arrived, two people had been killed adjusting the coal burners. Parts of the plant which should have been under suction were expanding like a balloon due to the pressure inside. I quickly realized the operators had no idea what they were doing, nor was the coal we sent the right coal for the plant. The flame was detaching from the burner and disappearing down the kiln, but within seconds came roaring back and hit the burners with a bang and caused all the ducting to expand.

I persuaded them to blend out coal with another coal and reported back to Calgary that the manufacturers of the plant had to be called back. It was dangerous for me to hang around there as I and more people could get killed, and the company might be blamed for it! The CEO agreed and told me to write a memo pointing out the problems and dangers, and to get out of there, which I did. I must admit, I was physically and mentally ill-prepared for this sort of adventure. The Philippines jointed Korea on my list of least favorite countries to visit.

Only two weeks after I was there, a massive typhoon blew in and took a large part of the plant to the bottom of the Surigao Channel. Not exactly the best way to solve a problem!

✳ ✳ ✳

Through some of my relations in the U.K., I got a cement company interested in buying coal from our Canadian mines and arranged a meeting in the U.K. The oil side got wind of this and sent a person from their headquarters in London to assist me. He had no idea about coal but was determined that nobody else would sell any sort of fuel into the U.K. and spent his whole time working on how he could stop a sale. Another factor to note about the oil company: People regarded the territory they were responsible for, as far as oil is concerned, as their private fiefdom.

I got a rest from traveling for a few weeks, but it could not last. We had got a positive response from the Portuguese government, and it was decided to send a vice-president and me to Lisbon in July. The vice-president was a stickler for dress and insisted in me wearing a white shirt, tie, charcoal grey suite, and polished shoes. He ordered me to come to the office the day before we were to travel, dressed for the meeting and carried out an inspection of me to make sure I was appropriately dressed. Both of us, dressed like tailor's dummies, went to the meeting in their head office. We were met by the Portuguese who were dressed in shorts and beachwear! They announced the meeting and lunch would be moved from Lisbon to the beach at Estoril! It turned out the restaurant was on the nude beach, and walking on the beach we were jeered at, called Jehovah's Witnesses, and had ice cream thrown at us. I never realized how much ice cream could ruin the look of a smart black suite. We both fried in those suites! We had to sneak into our hotel the back way afterwards, as even our trousers were covered in ice cream stains.

Later that year, I was traveling again to Japan. We had also sold a test cargo to the Tomato Power Plant in Hokkaido, Japan. I flew to Sapporo in mid-winter and arranged to meet our marketing manager at the hotel. It was cold at the airport and sunny. I was told the best hotel in Sapporo, The Grand Hotel where I was to stay, was only a short distance from the bus station in the center of the city so I decided to take the bus instead of a taxi. By the time the bus got to the center of Sapporo, it was blowing a blizzard. I was pointed in the direction of the hotel and told it was three blocks away. I started walking face into the blizzard. It was difficult to see anything.

What I wasn't told was the hotel entrance was on a side street. I must have walked straight past it as I had gone more than three blocks. I tried to ask people, but even as I approached them, they moved away. After trying three or four times, a voice from a big fur coat said, "Please come with me. I am going to that very hotel." She turned out to be an attractive Japanese girl, 23 years old, who said she had just graduated from the prestigious Pepperdine University in California and was on her way to meet her father who had flown in for a business meeting that evening at the hotel. We arrived at the hotel reception and were met by our marketing manager. I introduced the girl to him, and he invited her to have dinner with us that evening. She apologized and said she was having dinner with her father and business associates but would be staying at the hotel and would have breakfast with us in the morning at 8 am.

The next morning, as agreed, we met and went into breakfast. During that night between meeting her and breakfast, an event had occurred with our CEO back in Calgary. He had officially announced he was changing his name from Dr. James Green to Dr. Luigi Capoverde. So, most of the discussion at breakfast was on why a Canadian CEO would change his name like that. The reasons flowed fast and furious: He'd joined the Mafia; the Mafia were after him; some girl's father was after him, and so on. The girl added her ideas and some, if not all, were hilarious. Even though we were dining in the classiest restaurant in Sapporo, we were all laughing so much that we were in tears. At one suggestion, the girl laughed so much that she rocked back on her chair, fell backwards, and knocked herself out, hitting her head on the windowpane behind her!

Just as we and the waiters were trying to revive her, a group walked into the restaurant. It was her father and his business associates! They had a totally shocked look on their faces and immediately turned around and walked out! The girl recovered in minutes, and a waiter came up to her and said something and she excused herself and left. As soon as we had finished our breakfast, the *maître d'* came up and said, "We are sorry to inform you, but your rooms have been mistakenly double-booked. We have found you another hotel and all your belongings from your rooms will be moved to the new hotel." Well, we burst into laughter again! Later, the girl came to visit us in our new hotel and apologized, but it was we who had the most to apologize for.

On the flight back from Tokyo to San Francisco in first class, I was sat next to Henry Kissinger. He was one of the few famous people I sat next to on a flight.

The next trip was back to Korea, to a power plant in a remote area on the west coast in mid-winter. Our agent gave me a young and inexperienced driver who was scared of the large trucks. Halfway to the plant, crossing a narrow bridge with large trucks coming the other way, he panicked and hit the parapet of the bridge with the car just able to get off the bridge and come to a grinding halt. It was 10 am snowing slightly, and 23 F. He said he would fetch help and disappeared, taking the car keys with him.

The car got colder and colder and I got my suitcase out and put on as many clothes as I could. By 3 pm, I was really shivering and wondering about my alternatives. There was what looked like a hotel about a mile or so away across some fields, but the fields were deep on snow. By 4 pm and going dark I was really beginning to worry. The only Korean I knew was *kam sam nee da* (Good morning) and *wee hia* (Cheers). Finally, out of the gloom, a tow truck arrived and a car to take me to the hotel I could see across the fields. We continued our journey to the plant the next day.

The power plant operations manager was a very nice person affectionately known as Superheater Kim, since his initials were S. H. Kim. He spoke good English. Every single word I said, he wrote down, often asking me to slow down. Fortunately, their plan was to blend our Canadian coal with two other coals so there were no major issues. This was just the first time I visited the plant. On a later visit, S.H. Kim presented us with copies of his book called *Expert Systems*. It was a mixture of Korean and English, with every word I had said on the first visit written in it!

A company in Salt Lake City had heard of our problem and had a solution. They said they would give us a demonstration at a power plant in Salt Lake City. They started up the plant on oil and then went over to coal firing. I went to look in the boiler furnace and it was black! No sign of a flame, but still hot and the kept pumping in the coal. This is very dangerous, as it can cause an explosion and completely destroy the boiler. I dashed out and drove away from the plant as fast as I could. I got in trouble for not explaining the danger, which was obvious.

Chapter 15:
Big Brother Calls

The American side of the oil company decided to go big into coal, and had already bought mines in Illinois as well as Wyoming, in addition to signing an agreement with the Colombian government to build a massive new mine in Colombia. As part of this strategy, they agreed to centralize all their coal technical services in Houston, Texas and to provide technical services and training to the Colombian government. At that time, the main department responsible for the Colombian project was in Coral Gables, Miami, Florida while the U.S. operations were centered in Houston. The company's power generation business was also in Houston.

At first, I continued to work out of Calgary with trips to Houston, New York, and Miami, but slowly got dragged into more of the international work preparing for the big push into the coal market with Colombian coal. As part of the arrangement between my company and the Colombian government, I was loaned out for specific tests, particularly to educate their employees on coal utilization and head up test burns.

On my first visit to meet all the Colombian Project Team in Coral Gables, Florida, some of the team members were with me in the reception area of the hotel when our German marketing manager appeared out of the elevator stark naked! He was having a shower and went out of the wrong door in the room and into the corridor, with the door shutting behind him. He had very poor eyesight and without his glasses, he could not see where he was going. Apparently, he had to crawl on the floor of the corridor and feel his way to the elevator. What a great introduction to our German marketing manager!

The world had been divided up so that my company and the Colombian government's company had an equal split. This resulted in some odd things like the U.K. being in the Colombian government's area, and part of Spain in our company's area. There were also battleground areas like Germany and the USA, which was were not assigned to our company nor the Colombian government's. It was only a question of who got in first.

My first involvement with Colombian coal took place in 1984. This was before our mine had been opened and another coal was under the Colombian government's banner. The first ever supply of Colombian coal to a utility was to Thermoguarjia Power Station in the Guarija region of Colombia, only some thirty miles from our mine site. This coal came from the Prodeco Mine. It seems we were not the first to use this coal, as Sir Francis Drake's ships had taken coal from that region in the sixteenth century, using the area as their base during the attack on Cartagena was Riohacha (and Thermoguarjia was just outside Riohacha). They used the coal tar to seal their ships.

The test team was me, a Colombian representative, and an eminent boiler specialist, Al Duzy. He had originally been the Babcock & Wilcox head of engineering, but by now worked freelance. The original idea was to stay for a week at the hostel attached to the power plant. Unfortunately, Al Duzy was not in good health with diabetes, and needed specialist food which was only available in Barranquilla some 100 miles away. At the time, there was a major issue with FARC guerillas, and we were not allowed to travel to the plant after dark, as wire ropes were hung across the road between trees to deter the guerillas. We were not provided with a military escort, just a driver. This created a problem, as the average speed was 30 mph, with many security checkpoints, so it took over three hours each way to get there. As daylight in the tropics is approximately 7 am to 6 pm, this cut our working time at the plant down to nearly four hours a day.

The first day, I stayed at the plant while the others went back to Barranquilla. I walked down to the river, and suddenly there was a black shape sitting on a rock next to me. It was *big*, some 9 feet long and looked menacing. I literary leaped out of my skin, and did not stay to see what it was, alligator, crocodile, or lizard.

On top of that, we were frequently stopped at roadblocks by young Colombia soldiers who ordered us out of our vehicle at automatic-gunpoint and then had no idea what to do with us. Finally, they let us go on our merry way.

To cap it all, the plant could only achieve half-load, as the cooling water intakes were not far enough out into deep water to avoid picking up sand and blocking the condensers. The test was a technical disaster, but at least we got back alive!

I visited Colombia many times after that, and apart from being accosted by a woman in an elevator in Bogota for not speaking Spanish, most of the early visits went without incident. Some of my contacts were not so lucky and ended up as FARC prisoners in the jungle for a few years.

Finally, an early coal facility was built, which meant coal was available on the market but only in small uneconomic vessels. It was decided to send two test shipments, one Colombian government cargo to Crystal River, Florida and one to Studstrup, Denmark with my company's cargo. In both these countries, the authorities were very concerned with coal from Colombia and considered the ships a risk for drug smugglers. The ships were searched thoroughly and even had customs officials watching every ton of coal being unloaded. This was a recurring theme for the next five years with Colombian coal. They even brought in submarines to look under the ships.

My company and the Colombia government considered the coal to be the best thing since sliced bread. They confidently told me that once the coal was in the marketplace, it would go like hot cakes, and there would be no further need for my technical services. How wrong can you be! What they did not realize was the coal was almost pure. To them, that meant everyone would want pure coal. What they forgot is the power plants and others were not designed for pure coal, and pure coal would not work!

Once they realized this, they decided to add *overburden* which was mainly shale—a mixture of coal and other minerals—(but unfortunately, included some hard rock) to increase the ash content. The early coal was carefully selected and did not have an issue with rock. In the tests at Crystal River, the combustion was not great, with higher carbon residue than anticipated which meant they were not a resounding success, but no major red flags were raised.

Chapter 16:
Moved to Houston

Around this time, the CEO of the international coal and minerals was taken seriously ill, so serious that he had to take early retirement. A new CEO was appointed who was based in Houston and moved all the coal-related activities to Houston, including me! We left Calgary in mid-February of 1985 and moved to live near NASA in Houston in a hotel with outdoor swimming. When we left Calgary, it had been 0 F; in Houston, it was 68 F. We swam in the unheated pool, while the local Houstonians wrapped themselves in their fur coats!

When I first joined the oil company in Canada, they gave me an extra week's 'experience vacation,' so I started with three weeks' vacation. They also had written into my contract (which was still in effect when I moved to the USA) that I was allowed to use my frequent flyer miles for family and friends.

In Houston, it was vastly different. No Luigi, as well as not every third Friday off, and a boss who frowned if you asked for a day's holiday, who went over expense statements with a fine-toothed comb, and used statistics to check if too many expenses were ending in the same number of cents (especially 00c). He was frightfully conservative. If he sent an expense statement back, I just added an amount ending in an odd number, not just cents but dollars! He never questioned the increase.

Our team in Houston consisted of a former metallurgist who assessed the Colombian coal based on existing norms. He promoted the overburden addition idea and did the first laboratory size tests on the coal. He was a good technologist, but with poor interpersonal relationship skills—although you can't say mine were great at that time! He never got promoted and later took very early retirement after becoming bitter and twisted. We had an eminent coal scientist. He told it like it is, with no sucking up to management, but he was untouchable due to his high standing in the industry. Our coal quality specialist had his advantages, but was a bit of a brown-noser, always saying just what the management wanted to hear. Our other colleague was a chemical scientist and accompanied me on some of my trips. Our company also had a technical service person, a former marketer, mainly for the U.S. market.

The new CEO made it known that I was the only person he really needed in the technical department, which everyone, including me, was surprised to hear. This caused some animosity within the team. I don't believe it was because of my technical ability or my personality, but first of all, power plant managers—especially in Europe—had a deep-seated suspicion of former oil-based employees who had converted to coal. I always had an invitation to visit any power plant from the engineers at the power plants, but not always headquarters purchasing types, some of whom were even hostile. I was observant, extracting information from the engineers at the plants. I recorded their operational strategy, their future fuel demands, and their limitations, not just of our coal but also competitor coals, but also the amount of coal they had on stockpile, when and where their next shipments were coming from, etc. This was vital marketing information which the marketers could not get. Some of the marketers resented this, but most appreciated it. Some people called it spying!

With great fanfare, the full mine facilities in Colombia were opened. Our first cargo of 120,000 tons was a two-port discharge, first to the new power plant Moneypoint in Ireland, and then to Rotterdam for distribution to the Netherlands power plants. I was tied up with this shipment, so I never got involved with the Colombian government's first large shipment, which I believe went to France.

The test at Moneypoint went well. The coal was put on the stockpile first in order that the customs officials could look at it, and there was no sign of spontaneous combustion. Most of the coal was left on stockpile to see if it would heat up over time. The part that was fed to the power plant went well, but they had screens and it was noticed that an unreasonable amount of rock was separated from the coal, but this not a big issue at this plant.

A small amount of lump coal was screened from the cargo and presented to the local heritage steam railway for an inaugural run of a steam train carrying the mayor and corporation of Limerick to Donegal. I was invited to join them and was on the locomotive footplate for a short time. There were drinks at the bar in the train, and everything went well at first. Then the train started going slower and slower and finally stopped dead in the middle of a peat bog.

There were no mobile phones in those days, so they had to send a man up the line to a signal box three miles away, who ultimately managed to arrange transport in trucks. Unfortunately, the trucks could not negotiate the peat bogs, so everyone had to walk a mile to the trucks. I was not a popular person! It seems what ash there was in the coal itself, had a low melting point. On melting, it blocked off the air to burn the coal and the fire went out. They had to get a diesel locomotive to tow the train back to Limerick. So, the test ended up on a sour note!

I stayed in a hotel in the small town of Kilrush near the plant. I went to bed early on the first night I was there and fell fast asleep, only to be wakened up by a terrific noise in the street outside. It was 10:30 pm and pub in the hotel had closed but the people just carried bottles outside, drinking and shouting. At 1:30 am I got sick of the noise, so I went out to tell them to be quiet. To my surprise, it was the plant manager and all the workers from the plant and far from being quiet, insisted I join them. I was still dressed in pajamas.

While all this was going on, the ship had arrived at Rotterdam and had been discharged. A celebratory dinner was to be held a week after the arrival of the ship and the Castle de Rhon, a medieval castle, was hired for the occasion.

They were not too happy about the rocks on discharging the ship in Rotterdam. Some as large as a 10" x 10" when the maximum size should have been two inches. Even so, some of the coal was sent direct from the ship to barges to one of their power plants.

At the power plant, they had a 4" x 4" screen. Within two hours of the start of unloading, the screen was completely blocked with rock! The plant operators were mad, and we were red-faced. Even though the large lumps of rock were removed, there were constant blockages from the remaining rock. They struggled to maintain load. There was a discussion as to whether to cancel the celebratory dinner, but it went ahead with the plant manager making a speech. "You have a good coal <snigger, snigger> and we have a good plant. It's a pity they don't match up." We went away with our tails between our legs, insisting we would review everything.

Back to the drawing board! The rock was now unavoidable, but the size could be reduced by adding a new crusher to ensure no lumps over three inches were supplied. This meant we had to start again with our major customers and repeat tests.

The first test of the new coal was at Rotterdam. I stayed near the plant at a hotel called *T'wappen van Marion*. This hotel is famous for having the smallest possible rooms, just large enough room for single bed in one direction and in the other touching both walls and with your arms out. It turned out that my manager back in Houston had met his wife there, so they were actually envious that I had stayed there. Fortunately, there were no major issues with the rocks, although there was unburnt carbon which colored the white gypsum with black specs.

Numerous other tests were carried out in Ireland, Denmark, the U.K. Italy, Germany, Finland, and others, all with the same results. With effort, I found how to minimize the problems, but they never went away completely. For a while, I was sent with every shipment. Most of them were uneventful or had minor events. However, some of them were eventful, and not always associated with plant performance.

My first visit to Finland was one of the 'interesting' trips. I arrived at the airport and wanted to go to the toilet. The names on the toilet doors were only in Finnish, and of course, I chose the wrong door to the astonishment of the ladies there. I went to hire a car, and they told me to be very careful driving as there was likely to be people lying drunk in the road. Sure enough, even on the freeways there were people, mainly women, lying in the road. I had to weave round at least ten bodies to get to the *Kalastia Torpa* (Fisherman's Cottage) hotel.

That night I took a taxi to the center of the city and went to a restaurant which the hotel recommended. The restaurant was full, so I was sat by a waiter opposite a young lady. She never spoke to me but kept eating as well as ordering and drinking glasses of vodka. She did not look in a good way. She finished first, paid her bill, and left staggering somewhat. I left soon after and got to the taxi rank and waited for a taxi. A taxi arrived, and I told the taxi driver through the window where I was staying and got in. Much to my great surprise, the lady from the restaurant was slumped in the corner! I asked the taxi driver what she was doing there, and he said, "Oh, she was waiting for you to go to your hotel." WHAT!

I jumped out of the taxi at the hotel, but she followed me in. I asked the receptionist what was going on and that I had never said a word to this lady, and it was only that the restaurant was full that I was sat at her table. I left her in the reception, but five minutes later there was a knock on my door and on opening it, the lady pushed me out of the way, staggered to the bed, and dropped on it out cold!

At that time, vodka was cheap, and I was told it was a common problem especially with women.

The plant in Finland I was visiting was one of the most efficient and environmentally friendly plant in the world. Nothing was wasted. The plant had 1930s chain-grate fired boilers, but they were in series with back-pressure turbine with an efficiency of 86%. What made them super-efficient was the flue gas was brought down to room temperature by extracting the heat for sugar-beet drying, and the flue gas was sold as an inert gas to a local manufacturer, so there were no emissions whatsoever from that plant. The power was not only used in the plant, but also sold to the local power company. The low-pressure steam was used in the process of sugar and the ash used to manufacture concrete. Absolutely nothing wasted.

It shows you can burn coal in a green, environmentally friendly way!

Again, the problem came from the fact that the fine rock blocked the grate and reduced the air flow, limiting how much steam and electricity could be produced, so it was not a resounding success.

While I was working in Europe, my family came from Houston and joined me for six weeks in the summer. My former German girlfriend and her family came to the U.K., and we had great holidays in Shoreham near Brighton, Saundersfoot in Wales, and St. Constantine Bay in Cornwall.

Chapter 17:
The Colombian Government's Move into Israel

The first cargo of Colombian coal to Israel was supplied through the Colombian company and was arranged for early November 1987. I was instructed to accompany their new technical person to Israel. The first person who I had trained had left the company on compassionate grounds after his wife and eldest daughter were killed when the airplane, they were flying in from Medalin to Bogota, was blown out of the sky by FARC rebels.

I flew Houston-London-Copenhagen-Amsterdam-Zurich-Tel Aviv. Following meetings in Copenhagen and Rotterdam, I flew Zurich to Tel Aviv by Swiss Air in first class. About an hour into the flight, I was dozing when the cabin staff came round and said, "Put your seat back up and close your table." A few seconds later she came back again and said, "Put your seat back up, close your table and put your head between your legs NOW!" I was near the window, and the man next to me asked if I could look out of the window and see what was going on. We were coming down towards an airport, but it seemed too early and the airport too small to be Tel Aviv. I could then see the runway covered in white. A few minutes later we were told, "BRACE, BRACE!"

We came down with a massive bang with this white stuff spraying outside everywhere. As soon as we stopped the cry went up: "OUT, OUT do not take anything with you!" I grabbed my briefcase with money and passport in it but left everything else behind. They deployed the slides, but instead of being steep and sliding down, it was possible to run out, like being on an inclined trampoline. At that time, we had no idea where we were, and it was only as we walked to the terminal building and saw the illuminated sign reading RODOS did we know we were on the Greek island of Rhodes. We found out later that there had been a fire in the A320 cockpit of the plane, and the plane bellyflopped!

We were all shepherded into the terminal building, and it quickly became obvious we were not going anywhere that night. An hour later, we were told our luggage would be unloaded from the plane and hotels would be found in the city. Another hour later, and there was still no sign of the luggage, but a bus had arrived to take people to the hotels. I decided to get on the first bus and come back for the luggage. Most of the hotels in Rhodes were closed by then, but two were still open with a few tourists still there. I went to the reception, got a key for a room, and went and put my computer bag in it. It was a comfortably big room with the central heating on, since the temperature on the island was still warm during the day but cool at night.

I got the next bus back to the airport. By then, more people were arriving at the hotel from the plane. I picked up my luggage; by now the bus was full going to the hotel. At the hotel it was bedlam. People were fighting for room keys. There were terrific arguments, as many people were being crushed in one room, anybody and everybody thrown together. Orthodox Jews were placed with young American girls. Families were getting split up as well. I managed to squeeze past everyone and get to my room. As we had not anything to eat on the last leg of the flight, I went down to the restaurant which was still open. There was a fight going on there with Orthodox Jews insisting on kosher food. We were stuck for two days while they moved the damaged plane off the runway and brought in a replacement plane.

Finally, we got to Tel Aviv. It turned out that the new Colombian technical person was also on the same flight. The meetings went well, but many of the people were quite aggressive. There was a language complication as some people spoke only Hebrew, some only Russian, some only English; some spoke Russian and Hebrew, some English and Hebrew, and I spoke no Russian *or* Hebrew whatsoever. The Colombian also could not understand Russian or Hebrew and had limited English at that time. There were some slagging issues, but it was not possible to see in the furnace and we decided to have a second test (again) using my air-cooled CCTV cameras which I would bring from the USA as hold luggage.

Chapter 18:
Repeated Tests in Finland, Hong Kong & Canada.

We had not prepared to have two or more tests being required at every plant we sent the coal to, but that was what happened.

The plant in Finland had agreed to take a second cargo of coal on the understanding we had resolved the issue with fine rock, so once again I travelled to Finland. We did not have the problem with fine coal, but something infinitely worse! There was red wire sticking out from the pile of our coal on the stockpile. I went to investigate and too my horror, pulled out a blasting cap containing dynamite!

This was really frightening, as if this had got to the boiler… *boom!* I reported back to HQ but had to come clean with the plant owners. What should have happened was the army called in and the blasting cap disposed of, but in this case, the owners of the plant decided to dispose of the cap themselves and keep it quiet. We watched every pound of that coal which was sent to the boiler. They never bought any more coal from us after that.

An investigation took place. It wasn't the only time as blasting caps detonators had been found in other cargoes. It transpired that blasting charges were placed below and above the coal seams. It was always obvious when the top charge had blown, but it was not possible to know for certain that the bottom charge had blown. From then on, the use of under-seam blasting was suspended.

Still, even after that, detonators were found in cargoes. Even these should have been disposed by the army, but often they were given to us. Our notable German marketing manager had a drawer with them in in his office desk. Ignition wire sightings were common. Much later, the issue of blasting caps and rock addition dissipated as more coal seams were being mined which had more normal coal mineral matter.

By then, the second test of Canadian coal in Hong Kong was being carried out, so I had to fly from Helsinki to Hong Kong. The coal was more normal, but the flames were not stable and kept pulsing. The test was considered to be a failure and so no more Canadian coal was sent there. Instead, it was decided to send Colombian coal.

Just at that time, the airlines decided to ban smoking on flights. I was booked to fly back Hong Kong San Francisco and then on to Houston. A young lady sat next to me by the window. As soon as we took off, she started fidgeting and after another few minutes turned to me and said, "I am desperate for a cigarette, would you mind if I smoke?" I told her it was not up to me, but I would not spoil her fun. She lit up and tried to hide, but the cabin crew saw her and immediately came and insisted she put out the cigarette. An hour later, fidget, fidget, again saying she could not wait. She put a blanket over her head and started smoking again. The cabin staff were watching carefully by now and reached over and pulled the blanket away to reveal her smoking. The captain was called, and he threated to divert the plane to Tokyo where she would be arrested for endangering the plane. She said, "Right then," and took off all her clothes and sat there naked. The cabin staff said, "Just ignore her, do not even look at her." An hour or so later, she put her clothes back on!

I was able to get a few weeks at home and in the office, but it could not last.

This time, it was back to Eastern Canada. Our first shipment of Colombian coal was to Dalhousie Power Plant, New Brunswick. This plant, some ten years old, was selected to see how the coal would perform in the new Belledune plant being built. The test went well, but one evening during the test, the power was lost and everywhere was plunged into the absolute dark. I was a hundred feet up the boiler on a platform, in the pitch dark with the boiler safety valves screaming! I was unfamiliar with the layout of the plant and had to crawl on my hands and knees and try to feel for the exit and steps down to the next level. I was scared. It took me two hours to get to the ground floor and find the exit. Even some of the operations people had the same problem. That evening, we all went to celebrate our survival at the Canadian Legion where there was a dance going on. We sang and danced to 'appropriate' jazzed-up religious songs like,

"I see the light, I see the light, Oh Lord, I see the light," and "What a friend we have in Jesus."

Chapter 19:
The Notorious Traveler

By now I was travelling over the Atlantic or Pacific almost every weekend. The company's policy was to travel economy class on flights up to six hours. Above six hours, we were flown business class if available. Flights above ten hours could be in first class. The policy was not clear between six and ten hours, but it was usually possible to fly a route above ten hours even when the more direct route was less than ten hours.

First class seats were big and wide reclining seats, not quite horizontal and not like sleeper seats today. Business class was more comfortable than economy but did not recline much and had a poor footrest. Economy was slightly better than the package airline seats of today. Even so, I found it difficult to sleep in business class and impossible in economy.

Continental Airlines brought out their Business-First seats, but on my first ever flight using Business-First I suffered a herniated disk in my neck and had to wear a neck brace for four weeks. I set up my own designed traction unit on my bed and slept in traction for three weeks. My doctor was not impressed, as he was worried I might strange myself, but it did the trick, and I had no problems afterwards. On all the Business-First flights I was booked on after that, I was usually successful in getting the cabin staff to block out four seats in the middle of economy class and I slept full length. I even got a special seat belt which ensured I was strapped in.

I gained a reputation within the company and airlines for sleeping under the seat. Even our CEO knew about it, as he was involved with the airlines when they brought out a new policy that banned people sleeping under the seat. He said the airlines, especially Qantas and United, had mentioned me by name! Panam always upgraded me to first class... maybe that's why they went bust. Nobody could understand how I could even get under the seat, never mind sleep under it in business class *or* economy. Economy was difficult, but I could do it with less than an inch, to spare, as I am 5'9". In fact, I was asked to give displays how I did it to the company management.

For the next test, the coal was shipped to a deep-water port in the Straits of Canso between Cape Breton Island and mainland Nova Scotia. It seemed like half the Canadian military had turned up to watch the ship arrive. This included Royal Canadian Mounted Police, 1st Battalion Nova Scotia Highlanders regiment—with no pipe band, though—and a navy flotilla with a full-size diesel submarine, which seemed to be being used as an ice breaker as it was 0 F and there was some ice on the sea.

The hotel receptionist at Port Hawkesbury invited me back to her house. I had forgotten how primitively some people live, even in Canada. She and her friend lived in the forest, and my hired car with chains on just about made it through the snow drifts. She normally had to walk the three miles home from the hotel. The house was really a shack without electricity, gas, or running water, and had an outside toilet. It consisted of just a living room with part as a kitchen, a wood burning stove for cooking and heating, and a small unheated bedroom. There was ice covering all the windows and bone chilling cold inside the house when we arrived. I helped by gathering and chopping wood, and getting the stove going, as well as collecting water from an unfrozen well.

Three months later, the new power plant Belledune opened, and it was back to New Brunswick, still in the depths of winter, which seems to have been a reoccurring theme. Everything went well, except there was a real danger at their storage facility. They had an indoor storage area, a massive wood dome, the size of a football field and more than a hundred feet high at the center of the dome. Someone had forgot that coal from Colombia was 80 F and the temperature outside the dome was between 0 and −10 F in winter, with the outside of the dome being covered in ice and snow. As soon as a cargo of Colombian coal was placed in the dome, a fog set in in the dome and water condensed on the inside of the dome producing rain. The effect on the outer surface of the dome was even worse as it melted the ice on the dome surface. Sheets of ice started sliding off the dome, and by the time the sheet ice got to the outer wall of the dome, it was travelling at 40 mph. This ice, 4 inches thick and 30 feet by 30 feet, literally cut through the solid rock surrounding the dome and cut the wood shelter in half. The entrance had to have massive armor plating added to the wood structure.

No rest for the wicked! As soon as the tests were completed in Eastern Canada, it was off to Germany and another test there.

In 1989, I flew into Berlin. This was soon after the fall of the Berlin Wall. Even though the wall was down, and East and West Berlin were back together, it was two difference countries. I ate bear in the Café Moscow inside the old East zone. The whole scene reminded me of the Harry Lime film.

I carried out tests at many plants in Germany, most without any problems. Some were worried that the coal they got by barge was not of the same quality as the total ship's cargo which left Colombia, so a massive sampling and analysis program had to be carried out at every port or place where the coal was moved from vessel to vessel of vessel to and from stockpiles.

Our first shipment to Rostock, Germany, formerly in East Germany on the Baltic Sea, occurred within a year of the fall of the Berlin Wall. German Police were brought in with dogs to search the ship. The dogs hated going up open steps and smelling the coal. I stayed at a hotel near the beach in Rostock. It was winter, and most places were closed.

The hotel advertised that they had a swimming pool, but at first, I could not find it. I asked the reception whether it was open. The receptionist said, "Yes, just go down the stairs to the end of the corridor." I put my swimming shorts on in my room and went down with a towel. It was all in darkness, but I finally found the changing room and put the light on. Everywhere else was still in darkness, but I could hear laugher and chattering. Suddenly the door opened, and two late teenage girls came in, stark naked, and said in German, "You must be American. You cannot come in here wearing those things," and promptly ripped off my swimming shorts. They then said, "We'll take you in and introduce you to everyone in the swimming pool."

I found it really strange to be led in the complete dark by two naked girls to meet other obviously naked people in the swimming pool. I was sort of frightened to put out my hands, not knowing what I might touch. I did not feel comfortable, and after ten minutes or so I got out and found the sauna, which had nobody in it, and sat on a bench. I no sooner sat down when the two girls came in and put the light on. One of them stood on the bench, put her legs each side of me and started laughing and moving her private parts towards my face. I froze!

I did not dare touch her, as if she screamed, she could accuse me of sexual attack. She had a witness, and I didn't know anybody. Who would believe me! Suddenly, the door opened again, and a naked lady walk in, and the girl said, "Oh hi, Mom."

I shouted "Is this your daughter? Can you not see what she's doing!?"

The mother said, "Oh just ignore her, she likes causing an embarrassment, especially to Americans. She's just having a bit of fun!" Fun indeed! They invited me for a drink in the bar afterwards.

It seems there were a lot of women round there, some with children. The area was formally a STASI (East German secret police) holiday resort, and the STASI had their 'girlfriends' there. Once the Berlin Wall fell and West Germany took over and united the country, the girls were given the former Stasi houses and a pension from the state. The pool was kept in darkness, as the street side had glass windows. It was usually for 'dirty old men,' as they called them, to walk their dogs and peer into the pool.

Most German hotel swimming pools are nude or have nude sections. The Hilton Hotel in Dusseldorf is half nude and half clothed. I went swimming there once, and I was the only one in the pool. A guard blew his whistle at me telling me I had to take my clothes off as I was swimming in the nude area, which I did. I swam over to the other side of the pool, and he blew his whistle again and said this is the clothes part. There was an imaginary line in the middle of the pool: one side was clothed, and the other nude.

Following the first test and second test in the Netherlands, I went back many times to check on performance, but everything went reasonably well with only minor irritation and no major events, and we started sending coal to other power plants in the region.

A test was arranged for a plant on the Scheldt in the south of Holland right on the Belgium border. The Scheldt is the waterway to the major port of Antwerp in Belgium. The plant was a two-unit plant, one coal fired and one nuclear, with the turbines in the same building. Barges brought the coal from Rotterdam. During unloading the third barge a storm got up, first storm force 6, the 7, then 8. By then, barges on the Scheldt were disappearing under mountainous waves. The storm increased to force 11, the highest on the Beaufort scale, also known as Hurricane Strength 3.

Suddenly, the side of the boiler house cladding was blown off and landed on the terminals of both unit transformers. There was an almighty flash and crash, and all the safety valves blew making a massive noise and panic, especially on the nuclear unit. Everywhere was plunged into darkness, and it took five minutes before the emergency generator cut in. Fortunately, the control rods dropped into the reactor automatically, but it was a near thing. The third barge had sunk at the quay but was not the only barge to sink that day. The nuclear unit was brought back online first, and it was some days before the coal fired unit came online. Problems burning the coal paled into insignificance.

Some years later, I got an urgent call from our office which was now on the Belgium/Dutch border and was the old customs house. There had been an explosion at the plant on the Scheldt, and the plant manager was blaming our coal for the blast. Going into the plant, it was like a chicken coop. White dust and feathers everywhere, with no sign of the pipes carrying coal dust—the feathers were supposed to be used for an insulation. The cast iron pipes had been reduced to micron-sized particles. I spent most of the time reviewing the data and performing some coal tests and pointed out that it was an operational failure and nothing to do with our coal quality.

We carried out a test at a plant in the south of Holland. The plant was not designed for our coal, but surprisingly, it worked well. The plant personnel there were great and friendly but played a trick on me. They told me they would arrange accommodation for me and booked me in at a nun's convent! The convent dated back to the twelfth century, but also had one or two 'cells' (and that's the right word for them) for travelers as all abbeys and religious houses had at that time. It was really like going back into the Middle Ages. Stone floors, walls, statues, and no heating, although fortunately it was May and not really cold. Language, at least, was not a problem; the order was one of perpetual silence, and nobody was allowed to speak. The massive door of my cell was locked at 8 pm and only opened for morning prayers at 8 am. Breakfast in the refectory took place after silent prayers, and I was finally released at 9 am. No payment was accepted, just a donation to charity.

Chapter 20:
Australia
& "Schevenigeningen"

The company decided to expand their coal mine portfolio by buying a mine in the Hunter Valley, Australia. This mine produced both thermal coal and metallurgical coal, and suddenly I had to become involved in steelworks. Initially, this meant only writing reports, but it was clear I would be involved in visits to not only power plants burning this coal, but steelworks as well. As this mine was regarded as a competitor of the other oil company mines, the marketing had to be a separate organization and their operations, marketing and the coals' performance, kept confidential from the other mines. This was also true for the Canadian, Colombian, and U.S. companies so there was no collusion or co-ordination in planning work, visits, or traveling. Adding another company increased the complexity of arranging work, and especially travel.

My first trip for the Australians was to the major Netherlands steelworks, and I had meetings at the steelworks and at their headquarters in The Hague. I decided to stay at the Grand Hotel, Scheveningen. The hotel is one of the grand hotels in Europe but is now on the nude beach. I met two young ladies on the beach and got talking to them. They were completely in the nude and were more than happy for me to video them. On walking back, they asked me if they could come to my room and shower, as they were going to a nearby concert later. Getting into the hotel elevator, with the two still-nude ladies, I encountered—much to my horror—my next-door neighbor from *Houston*! Her husband, a colleague of mine from the oil company, had just been posted to Scheveningen for two years. Fortunately, she was quite accustomed to seeing nude people in the hotel elevator.

A year later, my daughter decided to go and study French at the town of Royon, near Bordeaux, France. Using my miles, she flew to Amsterdam, where I picked her up, and we later drove to Paris to meet her school class. My colleague in Scheveningen invited us to stay the weekend before I drove my daughter to Paris. The morning after we arrived, my colleague recommended we walk their dog on the beach. My daughter, clad in shorts and tee shirt, was absolutely horrified to see all these naked people on the beach. We had to walk the dog the next day and my daughter, dressed like a Muslim in a chador-type dress, could not bear to look at the people on the beach. Oh, American conservatism.

I was called to visit West Thurrock Power Plant near London U.K. by the Colombian government when the first shipment of Colombian coal arrived. The Colombian technical representative also came along. There were really no major technical issues. It was a good, trip and I stayed in London, managed to visit some of the nighttime hotspots, and go to three soccer matches. I always enjoyed going to the Café de Paris in Leicester Square and the Sacred Heart French Cathedral Crypt in Soho—NO, not for religion; there is a sort of church night club complete with bar and dance band.

Some two months later, I got a phone call from the Colombian technical representative to say a meeting had been called at West Thurrock to discuss the test performance. I really did not have time to assist the Colombians, as I had visits arranged for my other clients; however, as I was contracted to help them, I went along with their plan. I did not question why it was necessary and flew overnight as usual from Houston to London for the meeting. I arrived at West Thurrock in the mid-morning for the meeting. The plant manager said, "What meeting? We have not called one, and the Colombians have not arranged one, and we have nothing talk about." I rang the Colombian technical representative to be told that the meeting had been cancelled while I was in the air from Houston, and I could not be contacted, very strange.

This was not the only time I had a completely wasted trip. A high-level meeting had been arranged in The Hague between our president and members of the Netherlands government. There was a slight worry that a technical question would be asked, so I flew from Houston to Amsterdam on the overnight plane getting there at 8 am and went to the meeting at 10 am. I sat on the back row, never said a word, and at 2 pm, I caught a plane to New York and then back to Houston.

Two months after the first incident, I got another call from the Colombian technical person, asking me to go *again* to West Thurrock. I asked point-blank if there really was a meeting. To check, I called West Thurrock, and they said the Colombians had asked for a meeting but did not know what the subject was. I called the Colombian technical representative's manager, and he confirmed the meeting.

Once again, I flew again Houston-London and got to West Thurrock at the appointed time. The Colombian technical representative and his boss were there, but all it was all small talk: "Nice day. How are you doing? Is the plant running well? When is your next shipment due? Is the ship arranged?" and so on. I was completely mystified and complained to my oil company engineering manager that even though the Colombians paid all the time costs and expenses, I had three totally wasted journeys across the Atlantic.

My boss in the oil company decided to investigate this himself and insisted that I call *another* meeting at the plant. (Oh no!) Two weeks later, my boss and I flew Houston-London overnight again, and he launched an investigation. It was found that the technical person and his boss had their own agenda, a moonlighting business on the side. They were selling coal from other mines and had to be in London to sign deals and needed an excuse to get to London. Even though both the technical person and his boss's family had strong political connections, they were fired immediately!

My boss had never been to the U.K. before, so he insisted on a tour around London including shows and restaurants. I took him to Langan's (a very expensive restaurant owned by Michel Cane), as we were staying at the Intercontinental Hotel on Stratton Street, as well as one of my favorite touristy type restaurants in the dingy, former prostitutes' area Brick Street, behind Piccadilly, which is now an upmarket area. The restaurant had a good ambiance, served typical British food, and had British live musicians and bands playing and singing every night; one night was Cockney singers, another night troubadours, another English folk bands and singers, and so on. We also took in the Lord Mayor Show, when the new lord mayor is introduced to the city and the only time the royal coronation gold coach is used with the mounted band of the horse guards. As the following day was November 11th Armistice Remembrance Day with the major parade at the Cenotaph in Whitehall, London we went and watched the parade and saw all the British politicians and Royal family. My boss was exhausted after continuous site-seeing as we "crammed in" all the main sites in three days.

Before traveling to London, I had assumed that would be the end of my work for the Colombian government, but as they now had no technical person, I was told "Back on your bicycle." Oh no, not another person to train!

Chapter 21:
Hither and Thither

Back in Israel, they were having problems with rock again, so a Colombian government's commercial representative, myself, and a technical colleague from Houston flew to Israel. We were able to prove there was no rock issue but the meeting at the power plant was tumultuous, with people throwing things at one another and not really coming to any conclusion of what their real problems were, if any. It was mid-summer, so it was very hot.

After the meeting, the Israeli government's technical manager drove us on the main freeway into Tel Aviv. Soon, the car began to heat up. As we neared the top of a hill, we were in the middle lane and the car started to accelerate from fifty to sixty miles an hour. The driver took his foot of the accelerator to cool the car down.

Suddenly there was a scream from the back of the car where my colleague and the Colombian government's representative were sitting. They could see a cement truck barreling down the fast lane and moving into our lane.

The cement truck hit us on the pillar separating the front seats and back seats and bent the pillar. The car flew sideways in front of the truck. It looked like we were going to roll over. The tires flew off on the right side of the car against the road surface, and the windows shattered with the two people in the back seat hugging one another. The only thing I could think of a that moment was a Kenny Roger's song. "You picked a fine time to leave me, Lucile" and I have no idea why that song!

In what seemed like ages but really was seconds, we bounced free and flew down the fast lane going backwards, scraping the central barrier as we went. We finally stopped. Within minutes, the police and army were there. There was not a scratch on any of us! It seems that the pillar bent so much that the front bumper of the truck wedged together with the pillar and stopped the car rolling over.

The cement truck driver was Arab, and all the other truck drivers gathered round rather menacingly. I was due to fly out that afternoon, so the police put me in a police car, and they drove me to the hotel to pick up my baggage and on to the airport. My colleague ended up having to stay in Israel and go as a witness in a court case against the driver, who warned him never to come back to Israel.

✳ ✳ ✳

The Colombian government, now not having any technical person again, call on me to go to a plant near Oviedo, Spain. The Colombian government sent their ace marketer to meet me in Oviedo, so that he could be on hand if needed during the test at the plant. I flew Houston-Madrid-Oviedo and met the Colombian ace marketer. He seemed to know every girl in Oviedo, as every time we went anywhere in shops, hotels, or restaurants, girls would shout "PATCHO!" and come running to him giving him a big kiss. I now realized what 'on hand in Oviedo' meant!

The people at the plant were super. They helped in every possible way, including changing their operation to suit our coal and the timing of test to suit me. I wanted a small sample of fly ash left after burning the coal. After the end of the test, they presented me with a ten-gallon size, ornate, beautifully decorated, riveted copper milk churn full of this fly ash, far more than one hundred grams I really needed. They were great people!

The question was, how was I going to get it back to Houston? It was too big a diameter to fit in my cabin or hold luggage, and I asked for the advice of the Iberian Airlines staff at the airport. They advised for it to go separately as hold luggage and carefully wrapped it up in paper and tape with a label on it at my address, stating that it was fly ash.

I had three hours in Madrid before my connecting flight to Houston, so I was in no hurry to get off the plane. On the flight, now I think about it, one of the lady cabin staff paid a lot of attention to me, asking me where I was going and how much connecting time I had in Madrid. On arrival in Madrid, that same lady came again to talk to me. By then, everyone else had left the plane. I thought nothing of it, but as I walked down the jet way, two large men in Spanish police uniform came up behind me and smashed my face into the wall of the jetway.

They then frog-marched me down the steps to the apron where the plane was with the cargo doors open. There on the apron was my milk churn, minus lid, with the white fly ash spilt everywhere and blowing in the wind. *Oh no*, I realized, *they think it's drugs!*

The police said nothing but put handcuffs on me and we waited. Five minutes later, a truck drew up with three sniffer dogs in the back. The dog handlers pushed the dog's noses into the fly ash and the dogs howled in anguish as the dust got into their noses, mouths, eyes, and ears. They were fighting to get away from the dust. There were a lot of angry faces, they were sure they had made a big drug bust! Another ten minutes later, a senior officer arrived and a translator. "What is this?" I tried to explain, but they had never heard of fly ash. In the end, after maybe an hour, they called the power plant with the phone number I gave them. The power plant manager explained on the phone to the police what was in the milk churn, and they reluctantly took off the handcuffs and let me go. They insisted on keeping the milk churn and its contents for further investigation. Again, not happy campers!

As mentioned earlier, they had sacked their previous technical representative, so the Colombian government hired a wet-behind-the-ears engineer. This was the third person I had to train in less than three years!

As there were still some minor issues in Israel, we were soon sent back. This new person's family had 'escaped' Germany in 1945. Hmmm… they had obviously had some high position before that and were 'well-regarded' in Colombia government circles. This fellow was born in

Colombia and was very well educated and felt the coal technical services was not for him, but he liked the idea of traveling around and this was an excuse to visit many places.

On this trip, I took our air-cooled furnace camera and got some astonishing videos in the furnace, which prompted the plant to buy their own cameras. There were no major happenings, but we spent many happy evenings in the hotel night club. In the room next to me was the U.S. secretary of state, Alexander Haig, and the hotel corridor was full of FBI agents.

Our European Colombian coal office was located on the border between Holland and Belgium. Our marketing manager, who was single, arranged an evening with his new Belgian girlfriend, her friend, and me. He drove with me to Antwerp and left the car in a car park, while we walked to the restaurant where we were to meet the ladies. The meal started well, but halfway through, another lady walked up and started talking to us. She was smoking and asked the marketing manager's girlfriend if she wanted a cigarette. The marketing manager jumped up and said, "You used to smoke?" and immediately stormed out of the restaurant. I knew he was a non-smoker but did not realize he was vehemently opposed to any girlfriend who smoked or had *even smoked in the past*. I was left with the two ladies to pay the bill, and we all were none too happy. I found out later that the car park where his car was parked had closed and he had to get a taxi home.

We supplied coal to all the power plants in Denmark and I made some fifteen visits from 1986 to 1996.

On one such trip, I was in London over the weekend. On Sunday afternoon I had to fly to Copenhagen. I arrived at Heathrow airport nearly three hours before my flight and was asked if I was interested in catching an earlier flight which would be leaving in three quarters of an hour. Naturally, I said yes. The airline SAS said, "Oh, good, this attendant will take you through security control and take you to the plane." Very strange! This attendant whisked me through security and took me to a waiting car. The car drove to the edge of the airport to a Thai Airlines 747 Jumbo plane, and I was invited to climb the steps onboard. I was the only passenger! Something like ten cabin staff to look after me. It seems the plane had flown into London from Bangkok but was scheduled to pick up passengers in Copenhagen, flying empty between London and Copenhagen. As the flight I was booked on was over-sold, they freed up one seat by sending me on the Thai flight.

At Copenhagen, I went to the carousel to pick up my bag. My flight was the only flight on that carousel at that time, and I was the only passenger on that flight, right? Well, it seems not the only bag on the carousel, and the other one was identical to mine, so I picked it up and took a taxi to the hotel where I was astonished to find the bag full of women's clothes. I rang the airport, and sure enough, they had my bag and told me to come back to the airport to collect my bag. I tried to give them the bag I had, but they refused and said I had to deliver the bag to the lady at her hotel. They gave me her name, hotel, and room number. They added that the lady was fuming. I returned and went to her hotel. Fortunately for me, she was out, so I scribbled an apology and beat a hasty retreat.

The following day, I met the oil company's marketing manager for Colombian coal in Copenhagen and took him to visit the Danish power plants. On the way back, passing the Tivoli Gardens in Copenhagen, I looked in the rear mirror of the hire car and saw a car barreling towards us. I shouted to the marketing manager, but he tried to turn round and look just as the car hit us from behind. Our car was wrecked at the back and the marketing manager got a whiplash injury. We struggled to get out of the car and realized the gas tank had been split, with gasoline running everywhere. Even injured, the marketing manager dashed to the other car and pulled out the injured lady driver and her young daughter in the back seat of the car. The fire service came in a matter of minutes, and luckily there was no fire. The lady, who was Norwegian, admitted responsibility, but she had no insurance or a current driving license. The car hire company came and towed away the car and brought a replacement car. Fortunately, the marketing manager was not seriously injured, and recovered in a week or so without going to hospital.

Chapter 22:
The Crown Jewel, Australia

The oil company decided to further expand into the coal business and develop Operation Crown Jewel. This was so secret, nobody had to know about it. The infamous miners had found the motherload coal deposit! It was so sensational, they said, that it was a closely guarded secret. A deal was signed before we could even look at it.

This deposit was in Australia and owned by a company called Green Industries. Any name with Green in it immediately raised suspicions with me! On paper, Green Industries' assessment had shown the deposit to be fantastic and highly desirable... but had anybody checked Green Industries' assessment for quality? NO!

They had stated the moisture content was 13%. Any self-respecting technical person looking at their information and the information of the adjacent mine should have realized the moisture content available from a possible mine was 17 to 18%. At that time, 17 to 18% moisture bituminous coal was not salable in the international export coal market. The heating value had been also over-stated, so the mine could not be opened. Even worse, the deal included two of Green Industries' other operating mines, which had very problematic coals and a limited market potential. Talk about being taken for a ride!

The problem was dumped on our plate. We gave up on the Crown Jewel but had no option but to work on the problematic coals. Now I had three Australian coals to test as well as Canadian and Colombian coals! For me, it was back to the power plants which we had tried to burn first Canadian coal and then Colombian coal and now three other coals, two of which were problematic. I was getting quite a bad reputation in the power industry! Any plant which heard I was visiting knew they were in for problems!

We were swimming in coal marketers: three from the former Green Industry mines, one for the other Australian mine, four for Colombian mines, three for the USA mines, two for Canadian, and four Colombian government marketers. That meant that there was one of me, seventeen marketers, ten mines, and one technical assistant for the U.S. mines.

It was decided I needed help. The oil company brought in a technical expert from New York. He was a great guy, but unfortunately his wife was dead against moving to Houston to the point of way-laying our boss and physically attacking him as he went on his early morning jog! He soon returned to New York.

I was asked to go again to Israel, but before that I was to make a stop in Fos Sur Mer, France. Our Australian coal was a semi-coking coal and could be used at power plants or steelworks. There was a gap of five days between the work in France and a visit for a test of Colombian coal in Israel. My original plan was to spend those days in Israel and go to Jerusalem, but my oil company engineering boss (who was actually Jewish) frowned on the idea, as Hezbollah were active. I was instructed to spend as little time as possible in Israel. It transpired that I was the only person from the oil company who had ever worked in Israel, and I was only allowed to do that as I was travelling under the banner of the Colombian government.

I decided to fly Marseille to Geneva after finishing work at Fos and stay in Switzerland the four days before travelling to Tel Aviv. I booked a hotel in Zermatt for three nights, and the last night back in Geneva. I took the train to Brig, and then the track and pinion railway to Zermatt. I spent three wonderful days walking round the Gornergrat Glacier and even climbing up to the top of the Theodul Pass Glacier. I got back to Geneva feeling exhilarated, left my luggage at the hotel, and walked across the street, where I tripped and severely strained my ankle on a pothole! Passersby helped me back to the hotel where my ankle, foot, and leg started swelling like a balloon.

The hotel called a doctor, and the doctor gave me pain killers and ointment, and bandaged my foot up. I was told to rest and not move for at least three days! I was booked to fly to Tel Aviv the next morning! Frantic phone calls occurred with Houston, El Al Airlines, the Colombian representatives, and our hosts in Israel. It was decided that I should carry on. El Al sent a special ambulance to the hotel to pick me up and deliver me straight to the plane. The ambulance inside was more like an armored car, with an immigration officer in the front and two guards armed with automatic rifles in the back with me on a stretcher. I wasn't the first on the plane. There were more than six armed guards trying to look like ordinary passengers, strategically stationed in the plane.

On arrival in Tel Aviv, I was told to wait on board until all the other passengers had left, and another ambulance took me direct from the plane to my Hotel in Tel Aviv. The following morning our host arranged an ambulance to Rad Sarah, a clinic which dispensed walking aids. There they kitted me out with a leg brace, re-bandaged my leg, and gave me crutches.

On the whole trip, I hobbled around trying to teach the new Colombian hire. At times it was very difficult to move around, as there were open grating walkways in the power plant, and the crutches kept falling through the openings and getting stuck. The first evening dinner was at Mandy Rice Davis's restaurant, famous for the Profumo Affair in British politics. I had great trouble getting near to a table. Fortunately, I soon began to improve, especially when I could rest my leg in sea water on the beach. Flying back from Israel to Houston via Frankfurt, at Frankfurt I was told on my first ever mobile phone, to fly direct to Hong Kong, but by then it was too late. I had no alternative but to board the flight from Frankfurt to Houston and check on flights from Houston to Hong Kong. I was able to spend three nights at home before it was off to Hong Kong for a test of Colombian coal.

Again, they phoned me in the middle of the night the second night I was at home, and told me they and were expecting the ship in two days. The strange thing was, they were not sure where the ship was as they had not heard from the captain of the ship in three weeks. I took it easy getting there and arrived four days after the phone call. NO SHIP! Nobody had heard from the captain. A frantic search took place, but there was no sign of the ship. Suddenly, a day later there was a request from the ship for a tugboat and a small oil tanker.

It transpired that the ship had wandered off into the Persian Gulf to find a cheap source of fuel oil for its engines but could not find any and did not bunker up going round Singapore. They ended up running out of fuel in the middle of the South China Sea and drifted helplessly. Nobody was happy when the ship finally limped in five days late.

We had the same problem with Colombian coal at this plant as we had at others, and they demanded *another* test cargo!

Chapter 23:
Nothing is easy. Trip-Ups in Colombia and Canada

The Dutch government power company decided to send their technical expert to Colombia to assess the mines, and I was delegated to accompany him. The idea was that I would meet him in Miami, Florida and then travel by plane to Barranquilla. There, a company car with driver, also a guide, would meet us. We would at that point have escorts to the hotel El Prado in Barranquilla, have dinner, and stay the night. At 4 am the next morning, we were to be escorted to the airport by company car to catch a company plane to Puerto Bolivar, where we would visit the port. Then, after lunch, we would fly to the mine with an evening flight back to Barranquilla.

The Dutch government technical expert decided to bring his wife, and also wanted to visit another mine at the same time. My company would not accept visiting another mine. Even though the other mine was only thirteen miles away, the area was known as FARC terrorist country and my company considered it too risky. The Dutch were not happy campers right from the start, but it got worse.

The journey to Barranquilla was uneventful, but when we went outside the terminal, there was nobody there to meet us! At that time, it was quite risky getting a taxi, but there were three of us and no alternative. Sweating on the topline, we arrived safely at the hotel, found our bookings, and went to our rooms. There was still no contact from anyone, and I have very limited Spanish.

At 7 pm we went down to dinner. The Dutch decided they wanted to drink Geneva before the meal, white wine with the *hor dourves*, red wine with the main course, and cognac after. They proceeded to give the waitress the drinks list. Well, I had no idea what Geneva was in Spanish or if the restaurant had Geneva. To say the waitress was bemused is an understatement. Three people all telling her at the same time in English what we wanted, and she had no English. After about ten minutes she came back with cognac at which the expert's wife said, "No, no," waving at her to take it away. Ten minutes later she came back with red wine at which again, the expert's wife said, "No, no," waving her to take it away again. Ten minutes later, the waitress came back again with three glasses and... a bottle of red wine. Once again it was, "No, no."

At that, the waitress lifted the tray with the wine and glasses on it and slammed it down on the table, shattering the glasses and bottle and spraying red wine everywhere. She then disappeared, never to be seen again!

Some fifteen minutes later, a man in a dark suit came up to the table and just shouted "VAMOOS." We went to bed hungry, and the Dutch travelers were mad as hell, but I was still trying to phone people to check whether our flight for the following morning was on. At 2 am, I got a phone call back. I was told to take a taxi to the airport and the plane would be on time and they would tell us everything when we got to the port.

Naturally, we did not get any breakfast before we got on the plane, but they had realized we hadn't eaten and laid on a hearty breakfast at the port when the plane landed.

It seems a driver of a 150-ton truck had run amok and flattened the gate house and security building, and the army had to be called in to stop him doing more damage. It was only at 2 am that things got back to normal, and people were released to guide the couple. The trip to the mine and port went off without incident, but arriving back in Barranquilla Airport, the expert and expert's wife were strip searched in front of everyone. That was not the only time they got strip searched. The day after, they flew on a private plane to an air strip 100 miles from the other mine. They were strip searched both ways and had a terribly bumpy ride due to a thunderstorm. The joys of Colombia! They were absolutely livid with my company!

On Thursday January 3rd, I was supposed to have a meeting in Belledune, Canada followed by meetings on Monday and Tuesday, January 7th and 8th in Copenhagen and Kalundburg, Denmark, all for the oil company; then I was to fly to London for a meeting on

Thursday January 10th at West Thurrock, U.K. for the Colombian government; and finally, I was set to fly back to Houston on Friday the 11th.

Belledune is a difficult place to get to and the nearest airport, Charlo, has only one flight per day and that is from Montreal. To get to Montreal, I had to fly Houston-Montreal with a stop in Toronto.

The flight to Toronto on *January 2nd*, went off without any problem, but with a hold up in de-icing, the plane was thirty minutes late getting into Montreal and the scheduled connecting time was an hour.

Still, as I had only carry-on bags, there should not have been a problem *but* in stepped the French-speaking customs officer who insisted I empty out all my bags and examine all of it! I was very frustrated and must admit, I lost my temper. I finally cleared customs with ten minutes to go before my flight departure time. The airline staff said if I ran like crazy through security and to the other end of the airport, I could make it to the plane. I got to the gate just as the plane was pulling off the stand. I collapsed in a heap, but just then the airline staff said, "Oh the plane has to wait to be de-iced, so we will let you run down the stairs onto the apron and across the runway, and they will drop the stairs and open the door for you."

I ran again through the blizzard conditions and 14 F temperature until I got to the plane. By then I was really beat. In Charlo, I picked up my hired car and drove through a snowstorm the 19 miles to the Atlantic Host Hotel, Bathurst.

I slept well that night and got to Belledune at 9am the next morning, but I was not feeling great. At the meeting, it was like being in a sanatorium with everyone coughing and two people, the operations manager being one of them, coughing blood.

At 4 pm, I caught the plane back to Montreal Dorval but then had to commute to Montreal Mirabelle to catch to British Airways plane Chicago-Montreal-London Heathrow. I still did not feel well, and the London-bound plane arrived in Montreal two hours late… which meant I would miss my connection to Copenhagen.

I slept a bit on the plane, but just before arriving on Friday at lunchtime in London, I started having pains everywhere and difficulty breathing. I decided I could not go on. As it was now Friday afternoon, I decided to stay at our usual hotel in London, The Royal Westminster. I struggled by taxi to the hotel and got there at 3 pm and went straight to bed. I woke up at 8 pm in chronic pain, so I called the hotel doctor.

He said he could not see me there and then, but to go immediately to the Chelsea and Westminster Hospital emergency. He would warn them that I was on my way there. At the hospital, it was a like a zoo, as there was a flu epidemic, and it was below freezing.

In the emergency waiting room, there were many genuinely ill people, but others drunk or partly drunk, with two men insisting on being circumcised. I just could not help laughing, even though I was in excruciating pain. Many of the others were also ill but in hysterics at these two men's antics, with the nurses thinking it had become a mental institution. Seriously ill people were laughing themselves to death, it was like being in a pantomime!

Finally, I was examined and had x-rays. They said I had pleurisy and pneumonia, but they had no spare beds and even all the trolleys in the corridors were full, so I should go back to the hotel and stay in bed and take all the antibiotics and medication they gave me and come back on Monday.

Over the weekend, I slowly improved and went back to the hospital on the Monday. They said I was doing well, but would have to stay in bed for two weeks and should not fly for six weeks!

By the time I got back to the hotel, it was 3 pm, and near to the office opening time in Houston. I did not have the home phone number of my boss and my colleagues did not pick-up their phones.

I told my boss what had happened, and he told me the company medical doctor in London would come and see me. Later that afternoon, the doctor called and told me to continue the treatment and come at 9 am Wednesday morning to a private hospital opposite the Imperial War Museum, across Lambeth Bridge, and to bring my x-rays and medical records.

By Wednesday, I was feeling much better, and the doctor carried out more tests. After the tests, the doctor rushed in and said, "We are putting you into intensive care right now, but as there are no intensive care facilities here, we are rushing you into Kings College Hospital!"

I was quite flabbergasted at this, as I felt much better. Off we went with sirens blazing, and they put me in intensive care. After three nights there, they concluded that I'd had a micro-embolism.

It was decided that I should be moved to a better facility for longer term issues, so I was transferred to the Cromwell Hospital, South Kensington intensive care unit. And what a hospital! It was more like the Ritz Hotel than a hospital. It was owned by the sheik of Brunei, and my suite at the end of intensive care had four rooms. There were tailored waiters, a massive menu any time of the day or night, a wine list of twenty pages, and a TV with hundred or more channels, which was unheard of at that time. Nurses would visit any time of the day and night and even join you in a bath! Most of the suites had one patent, usually Arab.

After a week in intensive care, I was moved to the suite, given Coumadin/warfarin, and allowed to walk round pushing a frame with a drip attached. They said that as soon as I responded to the treatment, I would be allowed to leave hospital. One week and then two weeks went by with no response to the treatment. On the third week, I responded, but then they said I was on such a high dose, I could only leave when the dosage was much lower.

I finally left hospital six weeks after flying to Belledune, but that wasn't the end of it as I was still not allowed to fly. It was back to the Royal Westminster Hotel for me. After two further weeks walking around London, the company doctor in London, the Cromwell Hospital, and Houston agreed that I could fly home!

Chapter 24:
Dusseldorf, Germany, One problem after another, disaster in Hong Kong, 'swimming' in Ireland and fire on board in the Netherlands.

I spent four months recuperating from the illness and then it was off again on my travels.

I arrived in a hire car at the Steigenberger Park Hotel, Dusseldorf. The Steigenberger Park is one of the highest-class hotels in Germany, and I have stayed there a few times. The hotel has its own driveway in front of the hotel with two lanes. At the time I arrived, the inside lane was full of parked cars except for the space for one car directly in front of the hotel reception. The outer lane had a large fence and no footpath and no room to open a car door. I drew into the only available space and the concierge came to meet me, took my luggage and my car keys, and said he would arrange to have the car parked. Then he disappeared into the hotel.

At that moment, two police motor bikes came up the drive with lights flashing, and behind them came a police car, and then two Rolls Royce automobiles, followed by three other cars. One of the Rolls had a headboard and Union Jack, and this one stopped opposite my car. Everyone in all six cars tried to get out of the cars, but they could only open the car doors a quarter of the way open. All were trying to maneuver the cars so they could get out. After a few minutes two men finally got out of one of the cars and said to me, in English, "I say, you! Move that car!"

I said, "Oh, pray tell, how I am going to do that? The concierge has my car keys, and even if I had them, I can't move the car as your cars are in the way." At that point, a head poked through the window of the head boarded car and screamed, "Move that bloody car! I have to change, and my next appointment is in half an hour!" It was Princess Anne, the Princess Royal. Moving the car back and forward, they made enough room so she could squeeze out of the car with great difficulty. She was swearing under her breath and if looks could kill, I'd be dead. Finally, the concierge came back with the car keys with an assistant and organized the other cars to run around the block and make room.

A few weeks after my brush with royalty, I was back to Dusseldorf. This was my life, having to visit the same place just a few weeks after being there. It was impossible to coordinate work due to having too many masters.

We were attending a conference in Essen, Germany but decided to stay in Dusseldorf instead. A colleague from Houston, our German representative, a vice president (who was still based in Miami, Florida) and I flew to Dusseldorf via Frankfurt. The vice president hired the newest Mercedes sports car at Dusseldorf Airport, but he decided I should drive in heavy traffic to Essen as I was more familiar with the autobahns in *Nordrheinwestfalen*. My colleague and our German representative had an evening dinner appointment in Essen, so the vice president said he would drive and take me back to the hotel in Dusseldorf at about 6 pm.

There was not too much traffic, and the vice president said he would see how fast the car would go. I sat in the back of the car, but I knew something was wrong soon after we set off as the engine was whining, and as he increased speed it got louder and louder. I suggested that he slow down as there was something wrong, but he ignored me and sped up more. Halfway back, at near a hundred miles an hour, there was a horrible crunching noise and the car started losing speed. He managed to steer onto the hard shoulder where the car finally gave up the ghost! I then realized he had the car in second gear! He had never driven a manual stick-shift geared car before.

He decided to stay with the car while I walked on the hard shoulder towards Dusseldorf. I thought the police, or someone might stop, but by then it was going dark. I ended up walking eight miles in my dress shoes until there was a turn-off onto a secondary road. Finally, after walking another mile or so, I waved down a taxi and arrive tired, dirty, and with bleeding feet at the Breitenbacher Hof Hotel. This was another five-star hotel, but not as famous as the Steigenberger Park. I headed straight for the bar and nearly collapsed.

A well-dressed group of German and English people heard about my wanderings and said, "Oh, you really need a drink!" They ordered a cognac for me.

One of the women in the group said she was the CEO of a famous British fashion knitwear company, which was the same company I had worked at when doing my MBA studies. I replied, "Oh, I am wearing one of your pullovers!"

Taking my coat off she took one look at it and said, "No way, that's not one of ours!"

I said, "You're wrong, it is."

Sometime later she said, "Let's go back to my room and I will investigate further. If it's really one of ours, I will dress your bleeding feet." This got a round of laughter from the table. Back in her room, she took off my pullover and realized, after looking closely at the cut label, it really was one of theirs. Apparently, they cut the label of trial garments a certain way that are not approved for mass production and sale. She did not stop there but started stripping me and herself off. I never got back to my room that night, and in the morning only returned to collect my suitcase. She took me by company car to their private plane, and we flew from Dusseldorf to London. Another company car took us to Royal Westminster hotel in London, where she dropped me off. My colleagues could not understand why I was not at breakfast in Dusseldorf, was not on the plane to London yet, got back to London before them that morning and never used my ticket for the Dusseldorf-London flight. I never saw or heard from her again after that, except once on BBC news.

Three weeks after that incident, I was back in Dusseldorf again—the third time in a matter of weeks flitting across the Atlantic!

I spent the day visiting two power plants. That evening, I was invited to join the engineers in the *Altstadt*, the old wild part of the city. The bars were wild with drinking, singing, and dancing. At the end, a whole group of men and women said they were going the night after to a *Schutzenfest*, an old German traditional feast for hunters, in Neuss across the Rhine, and invited me to come along. It was even wilder, especially the German marching bands in gregarious uniforms marching outrageous goose-steps, with their feet being just as high as their heads. The audience roared with approval and some of the women were so hysterical, they looked like they were having organisms. (Hmm, Hitler would have been proud!)

I no sooner got back to Houston than I was off to Hong Kong again.

The company decided to pull out all the stops for the third test of Colombian coal. To emphasize how import it was, they sent the company's oceangoing yacht to take myself, the president of the power company, and my colleague from Houston from a pier in the center of Hong Kong to the power plant. The yacht was eighty feet long and housed the power company's boardroom, with at least thirty seats around the table. We made a royal entrance. They got the message; the results were similar to the first test, but there were no complaints this time.

Inspecting the coal in one of the holds in the 150,000-ton ship delivering the coal, we stood on the hatch covers. On getting off the hatch cover, a Chinese deckhand tried to assist me to step on a bollard, but he pulled me too quickly, I got one foot on the bollard but the other missed and I went sailing over the side of the ship, hitting the side, and dropping the thirty-five feet into the sea! Luckily, there wasn't a tender alongside where I fell, or I would have been dead. I ended up a few feet from a tender and they fished me out of the water. I was paralyzed and could not move my legs!

The tender brought me ashore and I was immediately rushed to hospital. In hospital, they did an MRI, one of the first MRIs in Hong Kong, and announced that I had not fractured any vertebrae but herniated three discs. They considered it would take weeks to possibly get me somewhat mobile again. My oil company in Houston, on hearing this by phone, announced that they had transferred me to another department three hours before the accident to ensure I would not blot the department's safety record... so much for safety records. As the company was the majority shareholder of the plant, it was a work-loss time accident.

Big discussions occurred what do with me. The final decision was that they would arrange transport back to Houston, but then I was on my own. The company would not arrange any medical help, make any recommendations, or do anything else, as it would affect their liability if I sued them. I don't know what the doctor in Hong Kong did, but I had no recollection of the life flight from the hospital in Hong Kong until the point when I laid in bed at home in Houston. There I was, paralyzed, with no help from the company and no doctor to go to.

Time for the yellow pages! I looked for sports injury doctors and suddenly I saw in a heading for 'space medicine.' This doctor and clinic specialized in back injuries partially caused by weightlessness in space. As I lived very close to the Johnson's Space Center in Houston, this clinic was very close, too. I rang the clinic, and they sent an ambulance and took me in to do an assessment. They did another MRI and other tests. Much to my great delight, they announced they would take me in right away and, more importantly, would have me walking in a week's time.

What a clinic! Once I was strapped in a bed, I did not see any doctor or nurse other than feeding, drinking, and toiletries, but there was CCTV on me from different angles twenty-four hours a day. There was also a TV screen and speakers in front of me, which barked out instructions and comments. The bed had movements as well as rollers which dropped onto my chest, stomach, legs, and feet. The bed movements were very gentle to start with but never stopped day or night. It was always gentle at night, in some ways aiding sleep, but during the day, the TV barked out instructions. For example, "You are trying to resist the bed movement. Go with it! You are not pressing on the chest roller hard enough. Keep pressing! We will tell you when it's enough!"

By the second day, I was sweating most of the time but not moving much. The TV kept saying, "You're not pushing hard enough, push harder!" By then, the rollers were irritating my sweating skin and cuts started to appear. I complained about to the TV and the reply came back, "It's to be expected." On the third day I was moving more, but with some pain. By now, my chest was red raw, and they bathed it with ointment and let me rest from the top roller for a bit. By the end of the sixth day, I could do sit-ups and press-ups and walk. By the end of the seventh day, I could touch my toes, which I could not even do before I had the accident. All the pain had gone, and except for being exhausted, I felt in better shape than I had for some years. They discharged me. I took it easy for two weeks, but still did exercises and was feeling great. Following a further three weeks without travel, the phone rang, and I was raring to go!

I was asked I could I get to Ireland immediately. A brand-new 150,000-ton ship carrying our Colombian coal was in danger of floundering on the Shannon River sand bar due to a severe storm. The ship had already lost its hatch covers and the holds were filling with sea water. If they managed to get the ship in safely, what could they do with the sea waterlogged coal? And if they could not get the get it in safely, what were their alternatives?

I dashed over Houston-New York-Shannon. The ship was still out at sea, rolling heavily. The waves were even going over the Kilkee Headland, which is at least eighty feet high. The biggest danger bringing the ship into the Shannon was the waves were so big that the ship might bottom on the sand bar and break its back. Leaving it out to weather the storm in her condition would most likely be the end of her and her crew. The ship headed in. The bow was thirty degrees to port; at same time, the stern was thirty degrees to starboard and kept twisting like a corkscrew. The ship did bottom out but only gently, and she slowly passed over the bar and into calmer waters of the Shannon, to a great sigh of relief from everyone. They even rang the church bells.

The ship was a real mess. The hold covers were gone, and the ship had a permanent twist in the hull, as the bow post did not line up with the center of the bridge or the flagpole at the stern of the ship. The sea water was to the top of the holds, and there was no sign of the coal beneath the water.

Our first job was to pump out the water above the coal… but how clean would that water be, and could you put coal-contaminated seawater back into a salmon river like the Shannon? Not only pumps were needed, but a filtering system, too, and that was just the start.

The operation was slow. Once we had pumped water out from one hold in the bow, we could start grabbing the coal from that hold, but to keep the ship trim the hold nearest the stern had to be pumped out next. Many samples were taken of the surface water from the holds and the coal, and the moisture chemically bound up in the coal. A mobile laboratory had to be brought in and operated twenty-four hours a day. It was not possible to feed the coal to the boilers in that wet state, and the question on everyone's minds was how much chlorine had the coal picked up from the sea water. Chlorine eats up the metal in a hot boiler very fast, and the coal had to be less than 0.3% chlorine (which is high for coals) to feed it to the boiler. The chlorine found in the coal samples was all over the map, from 0.01% to 0.9%. A space in the stockyard had to be cleared. Space for 150,000 tons when the stockyard already had 600,000 tons was a tall order but that is what happened. I believe it took ten years to ensure the chlorine was washed out and the coal drained down. They still talk about it today.

There were many problems with the coal sampling system at the port in Colombia. The design took an accurate but very large sample, which had to be reduced to ten grams per sample. This meant some fifty sample size reduction steps and all the time, the coal was drying and therefore giving an incorrect moisture analysis.

It was decided to change to a cross belt swing sampler. This type is normally used, but not on 6,000 tons/hour belts. The design worked well at first, but on the tenth ship cargo the sampling head was ripped away and deposited in the ship's hold.

Following further design modifications, I went to the port in Colombia to assess its performance. It just so happened that I was at the port in Colombia assessing a new sampling system which would hopefully avoid problems of bias when an event occurred. Ships came in and were loaded, but we did not pay too much attention to the ship's names. The ship that was being loaded was a Maltese registered ship called the MV *Crna Gorna*. After a new primary cutter was fitted and set correctly, the sampling test went well with no bias, and approval for continuous use was given.

Two weeks later there was a sudden flurry of activity over the ship. The ship had reached Rotterdam and a check had been run on the ship using a year-old Jane's list of ships. The year-old Jane's list said the *Crna Gorna* was registered in Yugoslavia; the name *Crna Gorna* is Serbo-Croat, translated in English as 'Montenegro,' a Yugoslavian state. At that time, Yugoslavian ships were banned from entering European ports. The ship was immediately impounded by the Dutch authorities until the ownership could be established. It was found that the ship was still actually Yugoslavian-owned and just using a flag of convenience. Flags of convenience were not permitted by the European Union for Yugoslavian ships, so the ship was permanently impounded.

The coal in it was still owned by my company, as ownership only passed to the customer over the ship's rail. The coal sat in the ship for six months and cost a fortune in demurrage. We were asked to help. What could we do? The answer we came up with was to *set the ship on fire* and get them to unload it as a safety risk. Normally we were asked to *extinguish* ship fires, not light them!

It took careful planning. The fire had to be enough to be regarded as a safety hazard, but not enough to get out of control and damage the cargo or the ship. We used oxygen sticks on the end of long poles with an electrical ignitor. We had both hose pipes and foam fire extinguishers ready. We had tested our procedure on a stockpile of coal beforehand. It was found that using water was best, as it sent up large volumes of steam, even from a small fire.

We carried it out just as it was getting light and called the local fire department. They came and used the fire hose and witnessed the large amount of 'smoke' (really steam), and declared the cargo hazardous, which allowed the ship to be emptied and regarded as distressed cargo. I don't know what happened to the ship in the end.

Chapter 25: Not So Easy

Visiting the plants so often, some of the power companies got wise to my visits, realizing I was obtaining vital marketing information. They started restricting the number of visits and insisting they had the meetings, one on one, at their headquarters and away from the power plants.

The company decided to get the USA technical services engineer involved in the plants outside the USA, and for me to get involved in the USA plants.

As an introduction, it was arranged for us to loan out our furnace air-cooled camera system to Moneypoint, Ireland and our USA-based engineer accompanied me to Moneypoint. At the same time, the Irish power company had new management and requested we put on a seminar for them at Moneypoint and in Dublin. The camera system was parceled up in large boxes and taken with us Houston-New York-Shannon as hold luggage. We plugged in the camera into a wall socket and *bang!* The transformer blew up. The system was supposed to be dual voltage 110 V and 240 V, but to our surprise the manufacturers had only wired it for 110 V. So ended our camera work!

The seminars went better than expected and were well received. Our group consisted of the marketing manager, the USA-based engineer his wife, and I. We stayed at the Drumoland Castle Hotel, visited Bunratty Castle and Limerick Castle during the day, and at night visited 'the sessions,' where people come in off the street with instruments and can sing and join the resident band for the evening at the Cloisters Pub in Ennis. At one of these sessions at this pub a few years before, I believe I met the now-Prime Minister of India, Naranda Modi, on an unofficial visit to Ireland.

In Dublin, we sampled the folk nightlife at various pubs with singing and Irish dancing for the tourists. There were some strange things happening at that time. The Colombian government decided to open their coal sales office in Dublin, even though Ireland was in our company's sphere of influence. The US engineer never did get involved in work in Europe, but it was a good trip.

Around this time, a cargo of our coal went to the plant at Kalundborg, Denmark. This was the last likely shipment, as the largest unit was being converted to Orimulsion, the mixture of oil and water being sold by the Venezuelans. Some of their older, smaller units were going to be shut down.

I took the plant manager to dinner at the best restaurant in Kalundborg, the *Ole Lunds Gaard*.

We ordered dinner and a bottle of red wine. We selected a bottle and the waiter brought it for me to taste. It tasted off. "No problem," said the waiter, and brought us another bottle of the same wine. It was also off. The waiter also tasted this one and agreed saying, "Let me recommend another wine," and brought a bottle of that wine. Same result. He went out and took the bottle to the chef who tasted it and spit it out. The chef recommended another wine and he tasted it and spit out that one, too. By now, the manager came and tasted another bottle, and without saying anything he threw it against the wall!

They brought in a big plastic lined basket and began throwing and smashing all their wine bottles they had in their wine cave. Needless to say, we never got any wine to drink! The food was good, though.

A cargo of our coal also went to Signeas Power Plant, situated at the southwestern coast of the island where Copenhagen is located. I got a call from the power plant to say they were having problems with the fly ash from our coal, and could I come and discuss it with them? They took me to the new bridge which was being built between Copenhagen and Malmo, Sweden. They were erecting concrete columns for the bridge and pointed out red streaks in the columns, which are still visible today. They had carried out an investigation and found the red streaks came for our coal fly ash, which was used as an add mixture to the cement. They then took me to the Power Plant where we saw red fly ash, and they compared it with fly ash from previous cargos which were all white in color. We did an internal review and agreed to selectively mine coal for them as they were a longtime, valued customer. By then it was Friday night, and I drove back to Copenhagen for the weekend, planning to fly to the UK Sunday afternoon for meetings in London on the Monday.

I was staying at the Hotel Admiral, which I did not like. In most of the rooms, they had very narrow single beds. I even measured my bed: It was 30 inches wide. Typical single beds are 36 inches wide. That evening in the hotel restaurant, there was a large party going on with free drinks, food, a band, and dancing. Two Danish girls invited me to join in. One, who was driving, decided to leave near midnight but the other, much to her friend's annoyance, decided to stay longer. We danced till three am. I offered to get her a taxi, but she said she would be happy to come back to my room and stay with me until I left on Sunday afternoon. Obviously, she didn't know about the narrow beds. I was not happy about this, especially with the narrow beds, which were impossible for two people. I spent the rest of the night on the floor while she enjoyed the comforts of the bed. By morning I had had enough and changed my flight from Sunday afternoon to Saturday afternoon. She was not happy at all.

As I mentioned earlier, our Colombian coal was nearly pure coal, and rock or overburden, as it was called, had to be added to ensure it met the specification of power plant boilers. The question was, how would the coal perform without the addition of rock? A test was arranged at a small power plant in Denmark with the coal screened in Germany and transport by truck. The test power station was unusual as the coal was pulverized at one location, and then transported again in sealed containers to another power plant where these very containers were used as their only coal storage. This was always considered to be very risky and needed inert gas to avoid fires and explosions. This plant was unique in another way. At this plant, there were *no* people! Everything was operated remotely from twenty miles away. There were no problems noted during the week-long test.

Chapter 26:
The Dominican Republic Hurricane and Japanese Trains.

We had sold a cargo of our Colombian coal to a cement plant in the Dominican Republic. As we had not sent our Colombian coal to a cement plant before, I was asked to go to the first use of the coal. Some ten miles from the plant was a holiday resort, and I stayed there. There was a mixture of Europeans: British, German, Danish, etc., and the rest from the USA. The attitudes to drink and sex were so different between Europeans and Americans. Most of the European girls were at least topless, some nude, and went into the bar in the late afternoon and plonked their bare boobs on the bar to the absolute disgust of the Americans.

On the second day I was there, there was a hurricane warning, and the hotel recommended that anyone due to leave in the next few days should leave immediately if they could arrange an early flight. Not many could do that. A hurricane force two was declared for the next day, and by the time it arrived, it was hurricane force three. My room did not face the direction of sea and it was on the second floor, so I was somewhat protected. The guests on the ground floor were moved up, and everybody in rooms facing the sea moved into rooms not facing the sea and doubled up. I had a family of four in my room. Nobody was happy, and there was little conversation. They placed the mattresses from the front rooms against my room windows, and for ten hours we sat there in the dark with the hurricane howling outside.

There was no damage to my room, although we could hear glass breaking somewhere. Generally, in the hotel, there was little damage. A few windows were blown out in the front of the hotel, but there was a significant amount of damage around the swimming pool. Palm trees had blown over, and even strapped-down tables had blown free and were lying in the swimming pool. Within six hours, however, everything was back to normal.

Outside the beach resort, it was a totally different scene. People were working cutting sugarcane with men with rifles watching over them. Back at the hotel I asked about these people, and they were most reluctant to talk about them. I was told the people who were cutting the cane were Haitians, and were held there in below-subsistence conditions, almost slave labor. They would be shot if they tried to escape. In the eyes of the Dominicans, they were 'sub-people.' The plant was grim, unsafe, and dirty.

Once again, I changed hats from Colombian to Australian coal.

I travelled again to Japan for our Australian arm of the company. I flew to Tokyo and caught the *shinkensen* (bullet train) to Kansei, where I was to catch a local slightly slower train. I was travelling with a young lady marketing manager from our office in Sydney. The *shinkensen* tracks are high up, and the local tracks lower down. A long escalator connects the two together. There were crowds of people, and I was carrying a large shoulder suitcase. Just as I started down the escalator, the shoulder strap dropped off my shoulder and went over the head of the escalator handrail and stuck fast! I was back-stepping like crazy but people behind me were pushing to get on the escalator.

My colleague from Sydney, who was behind me, realized what had happened and fought the people who were now piling up at the top of the escalator. A Japanese man also realized what had happen and grabbed my bag and gave it a massive pull. The shoulder-strap broke, and the bag was free… free to start bouncing down the escalator on its own. By then, the escalator below us was free of people, except for an old lady. The bag gained speed and, to our horror, bounced toward the old lady who was near the end of the escalator. Just at that moment, she bent down to look where the end of the escalator was and the bag flew over her head, to cheers from everyone!

We all breathed a sigh and staggered off to the local train. The train went quite fast at sixty miles an hour. The Australian girl said she wanted to go to the toilet. Five minutes later, she came back green and said, "I am dying to go, but I cannot go there, it's just a hole in the floor and the motion of the train keeps banging me against the wall." Hmm, another tricky situation! I have never before or since taken a young lady to the toilet and held her upright while she performed her natural ablutions.

There were always some odd things happening on the Japanese railways. On another trip, a marketer from Australia was with me, and we started filming people on the platform as the train started. A group of schoolgirls saw us and started waving and then running as the train pulled away. They were so busy running and waving, they ran off the end of the platform and our last shots were of them piling on top of one another at track level.

Chapter 27:
U.K. misadventures and St. Augustine, Florida adventures.

My mother, who was in her later eighties, wanted to go on holiday to a Methodist guest home in Kents Bank. Kents Bank is situated on Morecambe Bay, a branch of the Irish Sea on one side and the English lake district on the other. Morecambe Bay is treacherous, being almost flat sand with channels near the coast which all dry out at low tide. Being flat, the tide rushes in at more than 20 mph. The sand is firm at high tide, but as the tide comes in it turns soft. You can sink up to your knees and get cut off and drown as at high tide, when it is more than six feet deep.

My wife, two teenage children, and I decided to take her there. On the second day, Kents Bank had their summer festival day. The highlight for children was a tethered helium balloon ride and a ride on a tractor-trailer across the sands at low tide. The balloon was inflated, and three of the balloon suppliers' employees went to try it out. There was a strong wind blowing from off the lake district hills, which is unusual. The balloon went up about fifty feet and then a strong wind caught if and it dropped to the ground at great speed. After the weight of the basket dropped from the balloon, it shot up to another fifty feet. On hitting the ground again with a massive bang, the balloon supplier's employees were thrown out of the balloon basket. So ended the balloon rides.

There were many people at the events, and there was nowhere to park a car. The tractor-trailer for the children went onto the sands without event, but as the tide turned, it headed back into Kents Bank. The tractor-trailer was about to get off the sands when a parked car blocked their exit. This threw the trailer driver into panic as the tide was rushing in. Five other men and I saw the problem and decided to act. We picked up the small car, but the only available space to put it was the entrance to the women's toilet. I was the last to leave the scene and just then the owner of the car came round the corner. It was the Mayoress of Kents Bank's car! She immediately went wild and called the sergeant of arms and the police came and arrested me.

Fortunately, the five others who moved the car came to confront her. One was a high court judge at Lancaster, while three of them were JPs (Justices of the Peace), with one JP at Preston assizes, one Blackburn, and one Wigan. They ordered the police to arrest the Mayoress for endangering life with the placement of her car! In the end, everyone got let off with a caution.

Back in the good old US of A, we had supplied our Colombian coal to Jacksonville Electric Power Station, Florida, for a few years. This coal had been supplied to Jacksonville with many tests carried out, most of which were uneventful. Jacksonville announced they would do a test on our coal blended with petroleum coke, the residue from producing fuel oils. Pet coke is high in sulfur and vanadium, and a key part of the test was to see how well their flue gas cleaning scrubber could collect the Sulfur from the chimney gas when burning this blend. Generally, all went well, but there was a blue haze from the chimney. It was considered to be sulfur trioxide with the vanadium in the pet coke catalyzing the sulfur dioxide, which the scrubber could capture. Later, a special plant was added at Jacksonville to ensure all sulphur compounds could be captured.

As my company was supplying the coal and the petroleum coke, I was 'invited' (read: ordered) to go to Jacksonville. I flew to Jacksonville and the first three nights, I stayed at a motel near the plant but on the last two nights, I decided to go to St. Augustine, some twenty miles away. St. Augustine is a former Spanish colonial city, and known for its fort and attractive sea front. I had never been there. Before I arrived at the hotel on the beach front, I decided to first go and eat at a restaurant recommended to me by the Jacksonville plant operations manager, as it was already 7 pm. The restaurant was full, and I was asked to sit in a waiting area by the door until a table became available. Some five minutes later, there was a terrific storm outside with torrential rain. The people who had finished their meal and started to leave immediately went back to their tables and order coffee, meaning it would take even longer for me to get a table.

Another ten minutes later, a well-dressed, attractive young lady, about 23 years old flew through the doorway and into the restaurant. She did not have a coat and was absolutely soaked to the skin. She told the receptionist she was to meet a girlfriend at the restaurant, but after looking carefully could not see her, so the receptionist sat her on the chair next to me. She told me she had travelled twelve miles by bus to the St. Augustine bus station from her home and the weather had been beautiful and warm, so she thought she would not need a coat as her friend would drive her home afterwards. As she sat there, water was dripping down to make a large puddle on the floor. The receptionist kept looking at her and frowning.

I said, "Well, you can't sit there like that, and definitely not be at a table. What can we do?" I remembered I had my suitcase in the car, and she was almost the same height and size, but a bigger bust than me, and being the good Samaritan, I offered to get her some of my clothes as a temporary option. She agreed to try them, so I went to the car and pulled out a towel, vest, underpants, shirt, trousers, and socks and put them in a plastic bag. She then went to the lady's washroom put on my clothes and put her wet ones in the plastic bag. On close inspection, the shirt was a bit tight and revealing and the trousers a bit sloppy, but not really noticeable in the crowded restaurant. A table came free just as she got back and without any discussion, she joined me at the table and had dinner and a bottle of wine. The receptionist came again with a message from her friend that she had to turn back to her house due to flooded roads and could not make it to the restaurant. She offered to pay for the meal and the wine, but I refused.

Now what? She said, "Can I come back to your hotel and dry my clothes? By then the rain might have stopped and I can catch the last bus home?"

What could I say! I checked in at the hotel while she sat in the car and then followed me to my room. She put her wet clothes on the AC/heater and turned it to heat. She then went into the bathroom, showered, and put on the bathrobe. Much later, after dressing in her partially dried clothes, I drove her back to her apartment.

Chapter 28:
Let's join with the Italians.

My oil company's power division decided to have a close working relationship with the Italian National Power Company. My first involvement was a visit to their offices in Milan, which I tacked onto a visit to power stations in Germany and a power conference in Munich. It just so happened that a business colleague was also visiting Germany, so we both went together for the first part of the trip. After completing our work in Germany, I drove to Zermatt in Switzerland where she was so taken up with Zermatt that she decided to stay. I drove the hired car over the Furta Pass, through the Gottardo Tunnel to Lugano. For some unknown reason, the car rental company would not let me take the car into Italy, so I spent the night in Lugano, left the car there and travelled by train to Milan and back again the next day. As I had to go to Munich after that, I wanted to drive Lugano-Innsbruck-Munich, but that road has a ten-mile section which is in Italy. In the end, I decided not to risk it and drove via Zurich.

Our next joint project was a test at the Santa Gila Power Plant in Cagliari, Sardinia. This small power plant had been converted into a test facility for testing coal water and coal oil mixes. It was decided to test our almost ash-free coal in these mixes. The tests went well, and everybody was really friendly. I was asked to help a group of ladies who were going to give a performance of Irish dancing. Not that I have any expertise in the TV-type 'River Dancing,' as my only knowledge came for dancing at bars in Ireland and having once taught Scottish country dancing in my misspent youth. They were a great bunch, and we all learnt together. We practiced every evening of the week I was in Sardinia, but I was not able to be there the next week when they held their performances.

After a week in Sardinia, I was ready for a weekend in Rome, and joined a tour group—who happened to be mostly Korean Air hostesses—in touring the city by day and the night spots for the two nights I was there.

The next part of the joint project was visiting all the large power plants in Italy. I travelled from Rome by train to Genoa, visited power plants near there, and then went on by plane to Brindisi near the 'heel' of Italy. Then it was on to Trieste, then Milan, and finally plants near Venice, and another weekend visiting the sights. It was the Venice Film Festival, and I stayed at a Lido resort with private motorboat back and forward to St. Mark's square.

Sitting in St. Mark's square, a young American lady came to me and asked if I could help her by finding a drug store to buy some medication. She said she was on a tour of Europe and had been taken ill in Venice and was just able to drag herself from her hotel to St. Mark's square. The rest of the tour group and tour company had left her behind and moved on to Florence and then Rome. I went found a local drug store, but really no idea what her problem was and just assumed it was stomach and got some Imodium. I then helped her back to the hotel. The hotel was very good and said, "Oh, we have seen this before, and often." They rang a doctor and her insurance company, and before long she had the right medication sent up to her room. They arranged for her to stay at the hotel for another three nights and then to meet up with her tour group before embarking from Milan back to the States.

Chapter 29:
Wanderings in Malaysia
& G'day mate in Australia

At my office in Houston, my boss was head of the engineering section. Every one of my colleagues in this office worked on oil company projects. I was one of a few working on coal, and generally the only one involved with the customers power plants. My bosses, who frequently changed, were always bewildered by the range of activities I was called to participate in and could never keep track of my wanderings. As long as the mining companies were happy with my work, they were happy.

I had been visiting Malaysia for some years and established a routine with the engineers at Port Klang Power Plant. I usually arrived at Kuala Lumpur Airport early afternoon on a Sunday and went straight to the Kuala Lumpur Hilton Hotel. In late afternoon, I met the engineers in the bar and discussed the program for the meeting the following day at the plant. The engineers were nearly all ethnic Chinese, so they had no problem being in the bar or drinking.

On my penultimate visit, I arrived as usual and went to the hotel. In the late afternoon, I went down to the bar: NOBODY! I waited an hour, and still no one came. I went to the reception and asked if anybody from the power station had phoned to be told a person was waiting in the entrance for me.

The person waiting was a woman in a chador! I realized the lady could not talk to me, even look at me, or be seen with me without a male escort, according to Muslim tradition. I asked her if she was from the power plant, and she nodded her head. I realized this was the only way I could communicate with her, by asking questions. "Shall I recommend an agenda for tomorrow's meeting?" She nodded. I then went through all the items we had to discuss. Most she nodded except one where she shook her head. I wanted to ask why, but knowing I would not get an answer, I let it go.

At the meeting the following morning, all the Chinese engineers were laughing. They had played a trick on me and on the lady. She was a new hire. The Chinese engineers did not laugh for long as the Bumiputra, local ethnic Malayans, were slowly taking over all the duties at the power plant to the extent that on my last visit there were no Chinese, only Bumiputra, and the plant had changed its name to Sheik Abdul Azeez Kider Power Plant. On that visit, on the Friday afternoon, all the operators and engineers walked out and left me on my own with the plant still operating. They were all going for prayers at the local Mosque. I protested and asked, "What will happen if there is a problem?" The answer was, "It will be the will of Allah."

✳ ✳ ✳

Shortly after that trip, I was invited to attend meetings in Australia and visit all our mines. The first time was just before Christmas, and everyone was out in Sydney partying. It seemed strange to see people dressed up in Santa Claus outfits on the beach at Manley when it was 90 F in the shade. We flew to Newcastle and on to the Hunter Valley and then I flew on to the small town of Mudgie over the Blue Mountains in a two-seater plane. Back in Sydney, I walked over the Sydney Harbor Bridge from my hotel at Milsons Point in the evening. I passed by so many different scenes: wild parties in some streets, homosexuals in another street, and further on Aborigines, who did not look like partying. At that point, a man walked up to me and said, "G'day, mate, don't go any further if you value your life. Whites are not welcome, not even Brits."

On the way back to the airport after all the meetings were finished, the taxi driver suddenly stopped on the hard shoulder and ordered me to get out. He got my luggage out too. He told me it was the end of his shift and couldn't take me any further, but his colleague on the next shift would come along in a few minutes and take me the rest of the way to the airport. Later, I was told this is a common occurrence in Australia, and the locals do not get a taxi near the change of shift times.

On the flight back, I flew Qantas airlines Sydney to London, with a short stop in Singapore for refueling and then two days later London to Houston. I was in first class. Sitting next to me was a lady in her mid-thirties. She didn't say anything to me, but as we approached Singapore, she got up and went into the cockpit of the plane. Three minutes later, the co-pilot of the plane came out and sat next to me which I thought was really strange. I asked him where the lady was, he said, "Oh, she is going to land the plane in Singapore!" and said no more. Before we took off from Singapore, the co-pilot went back into the cockpit and the lady back to her seat. I couldn't resist and asked her what she was doing. She told me she was the Qantas chief pilot training officer and was on her way to a conference in London. She went on to say there had been a new protocol for 747s, and she took control of the plane and landed it to illustrate some of this new protocol! Hmm.

* * *

The first test of our new, *good* Australian coal was at the plant in Hong Kong where the oil company was the majority shareholder. A celebratory dinner was organized by our new wild, flamboyant Hungarian-turned-Australian marketer before the test for thirty people, including the power plant management and operations staff. My wife was invited too.

'Organized,' did I say? This man didn't even consider the need to book a restaurant, he just decided on a high-class restaurant and shepherded our group of thirty invitees in, then shouted "EVERYBODY OUT, NOW!" ordering everybody already in the restaurant to leave, most of whom were in the middle of eating their dinner! They were mainly Japanese and had obviously never ever been screamed at and told to get out in the middle of their meal, but they left! The restaurant employees were dumbfounded, and all the thirty invitees were gob smacked and horrified at this performance and even thought of leaving but didn't.

Afterwards, he somewhat forcefully invited everyone, including women, to the notorious Red Lips Bar, which was full of prostitutes, all over eighty years old! Hong Kong maybe unique in still allowing old licensed professions such as rickshaw boys and prostitutes. Lifetime licenses were bought in the 1940s and could not be sold or handed down, so there are still rickshaw 'boys' in their eighties and nineties who can hardly stand up, never mind pull a rickshaw. They just sort of stand there, looking like they are pulling their rickshaw, and get paid by tourists to photograph them. The same is true for 'working girls.' No new licenses have been issued, and motorized rickshaws known as Tuck Tucks are banned in Hong Kong and Singapore.

On my second trip to Australia, we ate at Doyle's on the water, and generally all went well. At the end of the visit, an Australian marketer and I were to fly to a conference in Bali, Indonesia. On our way to the airport in a taxi, a police car came racing up to us with his siren going and pulled us over. The police ordered the taxi to turn round and take us back to the hotel. I had no idea why at that point. At the hotel, the oil company's local manager was there to meet me and informed me that the Gulf War had started. We were forbidden to travel to any Muslim country. It took a couple of days to sort out new route and tickets and I ended up flying Sydney-Hong Kong-Los Angeles-Houston. I never ever got to Bali.

Chapter 30:
Lady marketer, Europe, going deep, and work in the U.S.A.

Generally, when I was involved in tests at power plants and working for the oil company, I was on my own. When visiting head offices, I was invariably accompanied by someone from our various offices. Each office had their own marketers or departmental heads who wanted to travel with me for their part of the program. I tried, not always successfully, to minimize the number of trips. This could mean someone from one office—for example, the Europe office—being on part of a trip, with other parts of the same trip having Australian and Colombian representatives. On two occasions, a young Australian lady accompanied me, once on a trip to Japan with other representatives, mentioned earlier, and one to Europe on her own. All other trips were with men only.

The lady had never been to Europe before and wanted to come with me on all my visits, even the ones which were not in her 'sphere of influence.' This was not allowed, so I had to concoct a program to dump her off at tourists' sites while I carried out the other visits. I had meetings in Frankfurt, Stuttgart, Milan, and a conference in Munich, while she had meetings in London, Frankfurt, Mannheim, and also the conference in Munich. This was not so easy. She had flown into London, arriving Sunday morning from Sydney, and took a leisurely tour of London on the Monday and then the meeting on the Tuesday. I met her on a Wednesday in London, and we flew to Frankfurt for a meeting where I hired a car. Late that afternoon she wanted to go for a swim in the hotel pool but was horrified at the nude swimming there.

The next day, Thursday, we got up early, drove to Rotenberg on the Tauber 100 miles away, booked in early at a hotel, and I left her sightseeing while I drove another 80 miles to Stuttgart for an afternoon meeting which did not involve her, then drove back to Rotenberg.

My program was to drive over the weekend to Lugano on Lake Como on the Swiss Italian border, and like on an earlier trip, catch the train to Milan for a meeting on Monday morning, while her program was a visit to Mannheim Power plant the following Wednesday. I decided to drive from Rotenberg on the Friday to Tatsch, Switzerland (near Zermatt), visiting the Rhine waterfalls on the way, as well as the Rhone Glacier and Brig. and stay two nights climbing round the Matterhorn Mountain. Then on Sunday, we would drive to Lake Como. She would spend two days sight-seeing while I went by train to my meeting in Milan, returning that evening back to Lugano. Then we would make the Tuesday drive to Mannheim for her meeting while I waited, and then to stay at

Rudesheim am Rhein. The next day, I would drive to Munich for a two-day conference, which we both would attend.

She was so thrilled at the Zermatt area; she refused to leave and travel to Lugano! Seems that ladies fall in love with Zermatt, as that was the second time a detour to Zermatt occurred. We arranged that she would stay at Tatsch till Tuesday and catch a train to Brig and on to Spietz on Lake Thun. I would pick her up from there, a really long way out of my way. I gave her my mobile number although she had not taken her mobile phone with her. I fully expected her not to be on the train, but there she was, and I drove her Mannheim. At Mannheim she said she wanted to spend a night with a friend of hers who had just arrived in Mannheim, and could I change the hotel to one in Mannheim? But of course that would mean losing the cost of the hotel in Rudesheim, so I said I would go to Rudesheim and pick her up the following day and meet her at 4 pm at the *Hauptbahnhof* (the main railway station) Mannheim.

I arrived at 3:30 pm and walked around the station for the next three hours! There was no sign of her! She had her luggage with her, so I decided to drive to Munich. *Just* as I was entering Munich, she phoned my mobile to say she had been delayed three hours and I should have waited, and by now she had had enough and was heading back to Frankfurt Airport and catching the first plane back to Sydney, and to hell with the conference!

Trying to organize trips involving more than one marketing organization's sphere of influence was always difficult. Either their itinerary's clashed or there were large gaps between appointments. As

I mentioned earlier, none of the marketing organizations were allowed to even talk to one another, never mind coordinating.

* * *

The oil company's representative in Germany and I were invited to go down one of the last operating deep mines in the Saar area of Germany. I have been down deep mines in England three times, as well as one in the Ruhr area of Germany, one in Australia, and one in the USA, but this was different. All the others were relatively flat-lying seams but, in the Saar, the seam was at a double angle some twenty-five degrees down and twenty degrees side to side; like walking down the side of a hill, but underground. It was very difficult to know whether you were at an angle, and even what was up and what was down. You felt like you are always falling and never level and always had to reach out for something: a metal support or a piece of rope or even someone else. To make it worse, there was little light from our lamps, the floor was deep in rushing water which disappeared into the abyss, and a cutter, bigger than a person, ploughed its way cutting the coal and depositing it on a fast-moving belt. There was a constant fear of falling into the deafening cutter. A real vision of hell! All the other mines seemed relatively civilized compared with this one.

As part of the change of work, with me working in the USA and with our USA-based technical advisor working in Europe, I went on two tests in the USA. The first was in central Illinois, and the second was in the northwest corner of Texas. We flew from Houston to St Louis and then in a commuter plane to Peoria. While on the ground in St. Louis, a massive thunderstorm blew in and we were held in the plane for three hours. Finally, we took off but hit the same thunderstorm and got bounced around like a cork in the sea. It was only a short flight and we made three attempts to land, dropping hundreds of feet with a lot of the passengers screaming. Finally, the pilot gave up and we landed back in St. Louis for the night.

Working in the USA was very different: there were no fancy hotels, just flea-bitten motels with the 'Good Ol' Boys' drinking whiskey in the bar. On one trip to near Laredo, Texas, my colleague insisted that I take my bagpipes with me. It seemed unreal, playing Amazing Grace in a Wild West bar. They did, however, appreciate hearing "The Streets of Laredo" on the bagpipes.

Chapter 31: A Sad Trip

A short time after my visit to Laredo, I was called upon to visit a power station in Wuppertal, Germany. There was nothing out of the ordinary on this visit, but I decided to phone up my earlier German girlfriend. I knew her and her family were spending their holidays in Switzerland, so I was not sure I would get an answer. Her husband answered the phone to say she had been taken ill and rushed to a hospital in Baden-Baden, Germany and they did not know what was wrong with her. I told him I would call back in two days' time, but also, I would visit her cousin who is a priest and lives in Remscheid, the next town to Wuppertal.

Her cousin told me she had very aggressive liver cancer and was not expected to survive more than a few days and was being sent home to spend her last hours with her family. I phoned their house and got her on the phone. She asked me not to come, as everyone was in deep shock, and she had only a matter of a few hours to live. We talked about miracles and said our fond goodbyes.

Her husband rang back two hours later to say that she had passed away. I said I would come to Stuttgart, but he said, "No, it is too traumatic." I sent a wreath and phoned again to their house but heard nothing back. In fact, I never heard from her husband or daughters ever again. No phone calls, no e-mails, no answer to letters. I did hear from the priest to say the youngest daughter had gone off the rails and she was a drug addict in a bad way, while the husband was now a recluse.

Chapter 32:
Bulgaria Red Wine Day

The oil company decided to expand into owning large power plants and I got involved in carrying out due diligence.

I was called on to travel to Bulgaria to carry out technical due diligence of three power plants there, as the former communist countries were considering privatization of their power plants and Bulgaria looked the best fit for the company. The company had hired a local company to be our agents, and this company was to arrange meetings, visits, and discussions with possible partner power companies.

The agent company sent me a program starting February 13th to travel by overnight sleeper train from Sofia to Varna. A female Bulgarian assistant and translator would accompany me. I objected to this, as I did not like the idea of traveling in a sleeping compartment for eight hours with a complete stranger or travelling by Bulgarian train at all. When I refused, they changed the program so we would meet at the Sheraton hotel and then fly the fifty-minute flight to Varna the morning fourteenth of February—Saint Valentine's Day in the Western world.

We met at the hotel. As we drove to the airport, a dense fog came down. We were taken to the VIP lounge where we were told it was 'Red Wine Day,' and they proceeded to give us glasses of wine. At that point, it was assumed we would not fly to Varna that day, but then gradually the fog lifted, and we took off three hours late. On arriving in Varna, we were met by a delegation who said, "Oh, it's too late to visit the power plant this morning, so we will go for an early lunch and… it's Red Wine Day!" So, we were given more red wine! Oh no!

After lunch, it was finally time to visit the power plant, but we were rather inebriated and climbing round the plant was a real effort. They then announced that the afternoon visit would be cut short and continued the next day, as it was Red Wine Day and there was a big feast arranged for everybody at seven o'clock that evening. After many toasts, we could hardly stand up. That was my introduction to Bulgaria!

As my company had grand ambitions to enter the power generating field in a big way, a month later, another trip to Bulgaria was arranged. I visited all the Bulgarian anthracite, bituminous, and lignite fired plants. My Bulgarian assistant set out the program and booked the hotels and trains, as well as a hired a car for part of the trip.

On a cold snowy day, I had to travel by overnight sleeper train from Sofia to Varna, Bulgaria. The first class train compartment was comfortable and warm, while there was snow in the corridor. There was a guard occupying a compartment at one end of the carriage where the guard kept the fire going to heat the carriages, and a toilet at the other end of the carriage. Outside, everything was deep in snow as we hurried through the countryside and reached near Shumen by four o'clock in the morning, some 200 miles from Sofia with another 100 miles, some two hours travelling, still to go.

I woke up and decided to go to the toilet at the end of the carriage, not bothering to put on a coat even though it was cold in the corridor. The toilet had also a shower in it, and there was obviously someone taking a shower, so I walked through the connection to the next carriage and went to the toilet there. I came out to find that the connecting door to my carriage had been locked while I was at the toilet! It transpired that I had left the first-class carriage and gone into the second-class carriage. I went to the end of that carriage and there was nobody; all the compartment doors were locked. At the far end of that carriage, the door was also locked.

We pulled into Shumen station. The train stopped, but the platform and the whole station was completely deserted, and nobody got off or on the train. I decided to jump out into the snow and dash down to the door opposite the guard's compartment, but before doing that I took precaution. I took the garbage bin out of the toilet and jammed it in the door to stop it shutting. I tried to open the door of my carriage, but no luck. I banged on the window as I could see into the guard's compartment and there he was, fast asleep. No matter how much I shouted and banged, he did not wake up.

Suddenly, the train started to move. I ran like crazy and was just able to grab the rail by the door and pull myself into the corridor. I stood there freezing for two hours till we reached Varna. As we entered the station, I jumped down on to the platform with the train still moving and jumped back on opposite the guard. The guard finally saw me and collapsed! I was told afterwards, once he had come around, he thought I had been out there all night!

I was taken on a tour of Bulgaria, mainly visiting all the power stations in the country. Our hired car had only three of its four cylinders working at times; it was difficult to get it to accelerate. We made our base near Varna at a small village on the Black Sea coast with beautiful white sandy beach. On the first part of the journey, we came across a group of girls linking arms and blocking the road. We were told to just drive at them, and they scattered. Prostitutes are supposedly banned from the cities, towns, and villages so they set up shop in forests at the side of the road and entice or even try to force passersby to stop.

At one power plant, we were being shown around by a manager when suddenly around the corner came two snarling German Shepherd dogs. On seeing the dogs, the manager took to his heels and ran like crazy. The dogs went right past us, chasing the manager, when from behind came a workman saying, "Oh, don't worry, the dogs have been trained to see off the management!"

Many other trips to Bulgaria were carried out, and we even signed provisional contracts for an office and secretarial services, but the Bulgarian government kept stalling.

Chapter 33:
Kranevo, Bulgaria, the Village of Cranes

I liked Bulgaria, as it reminded me of what it was like in my childhood. We set up base in a small seaside village called Kranevo. The Black Sea beach at Kranevo is almost white fine sand, and some five miles long. I was invited to buy many houses, most of which were in a very rundown state. Some were new but had very strange floorplans. Most had two or three floors, but the floors were connected by outdoor stairs, so for instance to get from the kitchen to any bedroom or living room, you had to go outdoors. This may be acceptable in good weather in summer, but not at all suitable in bad weather or in winter. Nearly all the newer houses were just *raubau* (they used the German word meaning complete foundations, walls, and roof, but no windows, plaster work, electrical wiring, main plumbing, etc.).

At that time, they were offering these properties at 14,000 US dollars which was very cheap, so I was very tempted. A person who we got to know offered a small plot of land 40 feet wide by 200 feet long almost on the beach with a 'house' on it. The house was unbelievable. It was built in the form of a boot, and was just like the old nursery rhyme, "There was an old woman who lived in a shoe…" The rooms had very low ceilings so I could not stand up in them. The second floor was even smaller, with quaint small windows in it. It also had a whole range of baking spatulas and cowbells, from very small ones to massive ones.

The cost was 18,500 US dollars, so I decided to buy it, knock it down, and build a modern villa. I went to Varna to finalize the paperwork and pay. When I was in Varna, the house was ransacked and anything of any value was stolen, including all the spatulas (except the biggest) and all the bells.

My assistant knew an architect in Sofia who was a well-respected artist, and she was commissioned to design the villa. She decided to hire a Sofia builder with great ambitions, as most Bulgarians have. The house was going to be in the form of a ship, and after getting the plans approved by the local government (with the *baksheesh, bribe*, typical for Bulgaria), the builder started work.

There was nothing but grumbling from him: The land was too wet, there must be a spring under the old house (which turned out to actually be a broken pipe), he could not get local workmen to work for him (the locals saw him as an interloper), and he was a religious fanatic. Every concrete pour, every brick laid, needed the local *Pope* (Orthodox priest) to bless it, and of course, everyone has a glass of wine. It was the Bulgarian version of the British comedy film *A Home of Your Own*. The architect was ripping me off, wanting $3,000 to connect into the local electric three-phase system. When we asked around, we got someone to do it for $40.

Finally, somehow, the basement and the ground floor itself was finished, but then the builder was not concentrating on the house, and the architect wandered off, too. We sacked the architect and builder and started again using the basement and the ground floor as the basis and hired a local architect who hired a *gypsy* builder. I was very concerned about this, but at this time I was on my travels around the world and really not able to control anything. Much to my great surprise, the architect designed the villa generally in line with what I expected, and the builder at first followed the drawings and producing a good quality building. He and his workmen had the problem of disappearing for a week at a time, which was problematic when they were in the middle of a major concrete pour, especially the main wall which was three feet thick, stretching from the foundations to the roof to be able to cope with a ten on the Richter scale earthquake. This took three months to pour. They never even cleaned the top of the first pour before pouring the second.

Again, much to my surprise, the villa was almost completed when the gypsy builder decided to go into politics as head of the Turkish Political Party. Most of the gypsies are Muslim of Turkish extraction and there are some 250,000 gypsies in Bulgaria. He was guaranteed a seat in the local parliament. He delegated the villa work to his brother, who was useless, saying for instance, "Concrete should be five parts of sand to one of cement!" From then on it was a constant battle, and even now you can see the wall surrounding the land where the brother took over. The wall is collapsing.

Some three years after the old house was demolished, we moved in. It is still necessary to line up to pay the post, electricity, water, sewer, telephone bills, and it takes a lot of time, as paying bills is a social event where the clerks discuss the usual goings on, "How are the family?" etc. with all the customers.

In winter it is quiet town of some five hundred people, including forty British, twenty Russians, six German, and four Norwegians. In summer, there are ten thousand people at any one time. Of those, some five thousand are Bulgarian, two thousand Russians and White Russians, a thousand Romanians, a thousand Ukrainians, three hundred British and Irish, a hundred Germans and six hundred others, Poles, Czech, French, Dutch, Danes, and so forth.

Many of the Russians, White Russians, and Ukrainians are children up to eighteen years old. These kids are known to drink a bottle of vodka each at one go! The teachers and supervisors have a rough time keeping them in check. However, they do not cause trouble. There is no hooliganism or sexual exhibitionism, other than not being able to stand on their feet.

The sea is deceiving. There are some rip tides in some areas. Nobody warns the kids. It is not uncommon to see a dead child lying on the beach covered with a blanket. Everybody just continues as though nothing has happened and there is no report in the newspapers or television. Just some poor parents back home in Russia left to grieve. Deaths are not reported. "It would give the place a bad name!"

There are many bars and restaurants with live music and dancing, both traditional and modern. They do not enforce a lot of the laws about drinking and smoking. However, they do enforce drunk driving (to my cost!). All the Russian, Belarusian, Ukrainian, and Bulgarian women love to dance and can get quite wild. In the earlier years, dancing went on all night, but now it stops at 2 am. The Brits can really drink, too, but drop out early and can't keep up the dancing.

The village center is less than a mile from the house, so I normally walk there, but on this occasion, I took the car. I also do not go to a Serbian restaurant, but on this occasion, I decided to go even though I knew nobody who was in the restaurant at that time. I had difficulty parking in front of the restaurant, but managed to squeeze in, although the back of the car was sticking out into the roadway. In the restaurant, there was a big party going on. It seemed to be a mixture of young men and women of many different nationalities. Somewhat to my surprise, they invited me to join them.

Some two hours and many bottles later, the traffic on the road cleared, as well as many of the parked cars, so I decided to straighten up my car. As soon as I sat in the driver's seat without even switching on the ignition, a policeman knocked on the window and ordered me out. I think he was just going to give me a caution, but within a minute, the whole crowd from the party descended on him shouting and pushing and he called up reinforcements on his radio. The reinforcements were not as friendly, and immediately forced the crowd back into the restaurant and brought out a breath analyzer.

I was unceremoniously put into a police car and taken to the police station. At the police station, there was much talking but all in Bulgarian. In the end, they took my driving license off me and took me home in a police car, ordering me to report back to the police station the next day.

Time to call in the troops! My assistant was in Sofia at the time, and she called a close friend of hers who was a lawyer in Varna, twenty miles from Kranevo. It turned out he was the police's legal expert on driving offences! He collected me and took me to the police station where all the police knew him. Back in Kranevo, we went looking for the people in the restaurant for witnesses and found them on a secluded part of the beach, guarded by the very police involved in my altercation the night before. They were porno stars shooting the last scenes of a porno movie. They were more than happy to be witnesses but pointed out they were due to leave Kranevo that night and had nowhere to stay. You guessed it! I now had porno movie stars staying at the house.

At the court case, I was given the lowest sentence possible: *no* fine at all and three months loss of license. As my residence card was issued in Sofia, my driving license had to be held in Sofia which had different rules. At the end of the three months, I had to go through a written, physical, and physiological test in *Bulgarian*. Fortunately, my assistant was a government accredited interpreter and translator and was allowed to translate the questions (and answers) for me.

In the last few years, the Russian Oligarchs have moved into Kraveno. They have built an Orthodox church, a 'Thermo Palace' with indoor and outdoor swimming pools, various hot pools, hot tubs, sauna, massage parlors, and a ten-pin bowling alley. I have only been in the Thermo Palace a few times. The first time I found the hot pool too hot, so I went into a hot tub. There was a couple having sex in it, so I was not welcome and went ten-pin bowling.

As well as the Thermo Palace, they have built an Olympic-sized ice rink and an Olympic-sized swimming pool, along with many hotels.

Most of the visitors are very friendly, but the Bulgarians are generally very miserable, at least in this part of Bulgaria. They are far more friendly in Plovdiv and Sofia. There used to be many friendly happy bars with singing and dancing, but for various reasons, these bars closed.

Most of the British are very nice, when sober. As drink is very cheap—for example a bottle of red wine can cost between 20c and a dollar—there is a tendency of people to drink too much. British tourists have a bad reputation. The Russians drink too much and easily get totally inebriated, but behave reasonably well considering their intoxication, while many of the young British tourists get drunk, wild, violent, and become sexual exhibitionists, having no thought about the people round them.

Most of the beaches are topless and many, although not quite all, nude. The beach lifeguards are as far removed from Baywatch as they can ever be. Most are men, also in the nude, in their late sixties who look like they could never swim more than ten feet.

There are many Russian women fitness groups on the beach, also in the nude.

We arrived once again in Bulgaria, extensively to sign a contract to carry out three-million-dollar study, preparatory to buying the power plants with the three million dollars contributing to the total cost of the plant. In between time, in secret, our company had decided to divest itself from all their coal-related assets, as well as the Colombian mines. We went into the meeting with the Bulgarian Minister of Energy and were handed a message from our head office to stall the negotiations and not to sign anything. We were not told at that time that the company was in the process of selling all their coal assets, but when the Bulgarians said, "Oh, don't do a study, just put a million in our back pockets and the plants are yours," we followed our orders.

We said, "Oh, thanks for your kind offer but we do not pay bribes and risk the company's reputation, especially to government officials in a country like the Republic of Bulgaria." Then we walked out! So ended our interest in Bulgarian power plants.

Chapter 34:
Craiova, Romania, and Dnestrovsk, Transnistria.

The oil company decided to look at buying power stations in Romania and I was asked to evaluate two plants. I was in Sofia, Bulgaria at the time and it was possible to drive to the plant some 150 miles, but the company insisted I flew to Bucharest first with a World Bank delegation. My company would not let me fly direct, as we were not allowed to fly on ROM airlines and had to fly to Istanbul, then on to Bucharest, more than double the distance and flight time. We stayed at the Hilton Hotel and had to fight our way into the hotel, as there were some fifty or so girls blocking the entrance. After going to our rooms, we decided to have a drink at the bar before going for dinner. In the bar, the hotel manager came in and recommended that nobody leave the hotel as the working girls outside were particularly aggressive that evening.

A Scottish man in the bar said, "Oh, let's find out how aggressive, I'll pick one out and bring her back in here." He went out and brought one in. She was none too happy, as she thought the Scottish man was taking her back to his room and started shouting, screaming threatening, and kicking out. The bartender called in the security, and it took three of them to subdue the girl and marched her off, we found later, to the lady's toilets where they strip-searched her. A short time later the manager walked in, carrying her underwear, and displaying them for all to see. She had double bras and panties. Between each of them were wallets, wrist watches, credit cards, and loads of bank notes of many different currencies. The manager saying, "What did I tell you?"

The following morning, we drove to Craiova power plant. What a site! Two units were operating, and there seemed to be as much fire, dust, and smoke *outside* the boilers. There were gaping holes in the side of the furnaces and red-hot lumps of ash and coal raining down, and yet the workmen just kept working with an eye on the dropping lumps and side-stepped the falling lumps, as well as the burning lumps littering the floor. We made a quick exit!

As further part of the move to buy power plants in the East, the oil company were invited to buy a large power plant in Dnestrovsk, Transnistria. Transnistria is a self-declared republic comprising of the Russian-speaking area of Moldova sandwiched between Romania and Ukraine. Only Russia recognizes it as a country, which was the brainwave of the Russian General Lebedev, who was at one time a likely successor to Yeltsin but was killed in a helicopter crash. Russian troops are still stationed there, supported by Putin. The oil company's power division decided to have a joint venture with the Italian power company, and we went as a group to Chisinau, Capital of Moldova, in an old Tupolev plane where the seats faced backwards.

In Chisinau, we were invited to go to a cave monastery. There was a funeral going on at that time. Everybody was drinking red wine, and the priest's horse ran amok in the cave with all the mourners chasing the horse. On the way back to Chisinau, with our Moldovan solicitor driving, we got stopped for driving the wrong way down a one-way street. As soon as we paid the fine and left, the police turned the sign around, stopping a car travelling the opposite direction. Everybody driving on that road was stopped and paid a fine for driving the wrong way.

The next day, we traveled by car to Transnistria where the border was blocked by Russian troops. They tried to question us in Russian. Fortunately, my Bulgarian assistant spoke fluent Russian, but they insisted on a thorough search of the car and luggage, as well as scrutiny of our passports and visas. Suddenly they realized I had a mobile phone. They had never seen a mobile phone before and wanted to confiscate it, but my assistant convinced them to let us through provided we went to the Ministry of Information in the capitol, Tiraspol, to register the phone. I have the first-ever certificate (embossed with the hammer and sickle) to allow the use of a mobile phone in the still-called, Soviet Republic of Transnistria!

The power plant is only two miles from the Black Sea but has no access to the Black Sea. The plant is massive with four six-hundred-foot chimney stacks. The stacks were part of the 1000 kv (kilovolt) transmission line from the Urals in Russia to the border of Bulgaria (most countries have only 400 kv lines and Texas only 125 kv. lines). The station employed two thousand people, but was not generating and in very poor condition, really only fit for the scrap heap. The people there were very nice and friendly and just wanted anyone to buy the plant and save their jobs. They invited us to be honored guests at the opening of their new Orthodox church.

We were called over to a garage (which seemed strange) and they took us down three flights of stairs under the garage to a massive wine cellar with thousands of bottles of wine. We tasted some of them, and the wine was fantastic.

We had no interest in buying the plant. When I got back, I found that eight hundred dollars had been charged to my Amex company credit card by a travel agent in Moscow, as well as one hundred dollars for the hotel in Chisinau. Two weeks later, my boss also stayed at the same hotel, and he got an eight-hundred-dollar charge to his credit card, also from the same company in Moscow.

We made another trip to Israel, and I was invited by some Greek friends to be baptized in the river Jordan by a Greek orthodox priest in a Greek church. I can now call myself 'Haj' instead of just 'Mr.'

About a month later, I had to attend a meeting in Sofia to set up an office there, but afterwards I was to visit a Japanese power plant for our Australian mines which the oil company still owned at that time. Our travel department recommended I use a 'round the world business class ticket, flying Houston-London-Sofia-Istanbul-Tokyo-Nagasaki-Tokyo-San Francisco-Houston. The conditions necessitated that I spend at least five days in Europe and Japan, which was no real problem. All went well until I got to Istanbul. At Istanbul, I checked in for the flight to Tokyo and they said they needed to look at my ticket and come back in half an hour, when they would give me the ticket back and a boarding card. Half an hour later, I went back, and they gave me a boarding card and said they did not know anything about my ticket.

What? I argued like crazy and met managers and other Turkish Airline representatives but had no success. The question was whether to board the flight without a ticket (and then maybe not allowed to enter Japan without a return ticket as well as the price of that ticket), or to stand my ground and miss the flight and the meeting. I decided to board the flight. They let me into Japan at Narita airport Tokyo, but with no ticket, I could not get on the flight to Nagasaki and had to get a hotel for the night. I made frantic phone calls to the Australian colleagues I was to meet in Nagasaki and to the travel department in Houston. The travel department were quite relaxed about it all and immediately arranged for me to pick up a completely new ticket at Haneda airport the next morning before boarding the plane to Nagasaki. It was a bit of a rush to make the ferry in Nagasaki to the outlying island where the power plant was, but we made the meeting just in time. I have no idea how the ticket issue was resolved; I was just told to "move on."

Chapter 35:
The end of coal, Re-training for El Salvador, and Change of Employment.

The oil company decided to exit to coal business, first selling the USA Powder River Basin assets, then the Australian coal asset then the Colombian mine and years later, the Illinois assets. The company let it be known they would keep me on, but in what capacity, as I had never been involved in the oil or gas side of the company? At that time, the company was keeping their share of the power generation in Hong Kong who were adding a very large environmental improvement program and a project manager's position was hinted at but not officially offered.

However, a week later, the oil company decided to 're-train' me to be project manager of a new diesel power plant being proposed for El Salvador. I was first sent to El Salvador to see existing diesel power plants. What was strange about these power plants was they had fifty-foot high, wire mesh fences round each plant. I was told the fences were to protect the plant from Rocket Propelled Grenades, (RPGs) as there were, earlier, armed rebels all over El Salvador. Hmmm.

I was also sent on two trips to understand the design and operation of very large diesel engines. The first trip was to visit the manufacturers of these engines. The main manufacturers of diesel engines are WARTSILA, Hanko, Finland for four stroke engines and MAN-B&W, two stroke engines, MAN in Nuremburg. Germany and BURMEISTER & WAIN in Copenhagen, Denmark. These companies manufacture nearly all the large diesel in the world, used for power plants and large ship engines. These engines are massive with twelve cylinders each with each cylinder wide enough and long enough, a person can easily fit inside each cylinder, interesting but no unusual 'turn of events' on these visits.

The second trip was infinitely more exciting. Three weeks visiting diesel power plants on the Caribbean Islands as well as Central America, while traveling there by cruise ships and discussing engine operation, maintenance, and performance with their crews. I visited Barbados, St. Lucia, Guadeloupe, Puerto Rico, Dominican Republic, Jamaica, Cayman Islands as well as Panama, Costa Rica, Nicaragua, and Guatemala. The engine manufacturers always wanted me to travel on ships powered by their engines and sent at least one, sometimes two people from each company to accompany me on the cruise ships. At first, I could not understand it. Cruise passengers were regarding me with "reverence." I asked a young lady who was particularly sub-servant, "why this attitude." She said, "Oh you must be someone very important as you have two 'minders' wherever you go!" Even on the beach in the Cayman Islands, there was an *entourage* round me at a discrete distance.

Apart from German Power Plant conferences, this was the only time I needed a "penguin suit" (dinner suit) at any involvement with power plants. After serious consideration, I decided diesel engines where not in my future plans.

Some of the customers who I had been involved with in some countries had joined an American Power company and were expanding into the international power trade. They invited me to join them as a consultant. My last month with the oil company was filled with two major retirement parties and a vacation. That same month, I started as a consultant with the power company. Initially, the main thrust for me was to assist three large UK power companies to increase their scope for other fuels than British coal, which they had been burning for the past twenty or thirty years and which their plants had been designed for. The British mines were unprofitable and were being closed. Imported coals were being considered as they were less expensive and produced lower gas emissions, which could be regarded as potentially harmful to the environment.

A program was envisaged for these three power plants to test, under safe conditions, a wide range of fuels which were outside the design range of the plants. There was reluctance from some of the operations personnel, but in general, there was acceptance as it was the only way to stay in business.

This involved a significant amount of work and involved nearly two years residing, on and off, in the UK again. I set up a UK company, but my official residence was still the state of Texas, USA, which meant that I was paying taxes in both countries.

We set up our bases at attractive historic cities, mainly Chester and York. In Chester we stayed at the old recorder's house, now a hotel. It was a house built in Elizabethan times with four-poster beds. The rooms face the Dee River, and the floors sloped towards the river. You always had the feeling that you were going to slide out of bed, through the window, and into the Dee.

In York, our base was the Marriott hotel. We realized we had to make frequent trips, as we were also directly employed as consultants by the largest power station in Europe. We spent twelve months at this hotel during a three-year period, and as we were regular customers, we were given a suite of rooms for the same price as a double room.

In York, our favorite restaurant was the Blue Bicycle. Sad to say later, as mentioned earlier, this succumbed to flooding and is no longer a restaurant.

We had already been involved in widening their coal quality specification and started testing coals from all parts of the world: Indonesia, Australia, South Africa, Russia, Canada, Colombia, Venezuela, and USA. Later, we also tested pet coke and Biomass.

On the first test under this arrangement, my Bulgarian assistant was in the control room while I was in the plant. When I got back, she said to me, "This operator keeps saying *you need sex*," so I went to listen. He was actually answering the telephone and saying in a local dialect, "Unit Six." When I told this to the operators, they put up a sign reading, "You Need Sex."

Thanks to the unit operators and all the staff at the plant, we were able convince them to accept a very wide range of fuels, which were out of the question a few years earlier.

We were also able to visit my mother in an old people's home almost every week and frequently took my first girlfriend's father out to dinner, as I was indebted to him for assisting me when my father was in hospital.

As the environmental emission limits became stricter and stricter, we had to move away from bituminous coals, first to sub-bituminous coal and then later, to biomass. With both these last two fuels, enhanced safety procedures were necessary. Courses were arranged, and it was necessary to have a safety passport before you could even get on the power plant site. These were updated frequently, sometimes without warning.

One day I arrived on site and was stopped and told I had to take a 'safe walking course': make sure you put one foot in front of the other, always hold the handrail when going up and down stairs, etc.

Another time I was stopped and asked, "Are you wearing your fireproof underwear?" It is now mandated as well as the other PPE

(Personnel Protection Equipment) including a hard hat, regulation safety glasses, regulation ear protection, full fireproof coveralls, heat resisting gloves, and hard toed shoes. They told me where I could buy fireproof underwear, but luckily did not insist on inspecting them every time I entered the site.

Chapter 36:
The Eagle Has Landed

For this trip, I was working for the new power company. Work was mostly at the power plants I had already worked at, and I was requested to attend tests in Nova Scotia, Canada. I flew to Halifax, hired a car, and drove the 100 miles to Cape Breton Island and Port Hawkesbury. The weather was good, reasonably warm for September, and it was starting to go dark as I headed up past Windsor. As I entered an area of rolling hills, I saw a black shape in the road. Cars in front of me were detouring round it. At first, I thought it was a tire from a truck but as I got nearer, it started to move. It was a bear!

I slowed down and tried to pass it on the other side of the road, but it lurched at me just as I was passing and bumped into me. I thought about stopping, but what could I do? I decided to drive on to New Glasgow and tell the RCMP (Mounted Police). They said I was not the first person to hit it and report it, and an animal welfare officer was on his way to tranquilize the bear and collect it.

I got to the hotel, and the following morning headed to the power plant on a minor road. The ship had not yet arrived so after lunch I drove back towards the hotel. I had the driver's side window shut and the passenger side window open and doing fifty miles an hour. Suddenly there was a mighty bang, and something hit me on the head and immediately after, I couldn't see. I was able to brake and slow the car down until I came to a stop in the middle of the road. At that point I realized there was blood running down my face. Was it my blood? I managed to wipe the blood from my eyes but still could not see out of the car as the front windscreen was also covered in blood. I then looked at the passenger seat; it was an absolute wreck, the back of the seat torn to shreds.

I cleaned an area of the windscreen and drove off to the side of the road. It was unbelievable. Torn seats, blood everywhere and then I noticed a claw, then a leg and then at the other side of the car was part of a rabbit and the head of an eagle! There was mashed up tissue which I assumed was the body, or part of the body of the eagle. There were signs on the passenger door with the open window the eagle had flown into the car. From what I could put together, the eagle had swooped down on a rabbit at the side of the road and was starting to fly off but flew straight through the open window of the car.

What to do? I drove slowly back to the hotel and got some old towels from the reception and dipped them in water and washed the windows so I could see out to drive. I went to my room, had a shower, and changed clothes, decided to drive back to the car hire office at the airport and put my suite case in the trunk of the car as I would most likely have to spend the night in Halifax.

The car hire people had never seen anything like it and called the press to photograph it. After filling in the forms, they provided me with a new car. It was now late in the afternoon, so I decided to phone my former colleague I had worked with earlier in Nova Scotia who now lived in Dartmouth across the harbor from Halifax. He told me to come to his house and I could stay the night and drive back the next day. He explained that he was working on his car in his garage but would be finished by the time I got to his house.

I knew the way to his house, so off I went. Halfway there, two fire trucks came racing passed me. When I got to his house, it was on fire from end to end! The fire brigade had given up on it and were just trying to stop the fire spreading to the next-door houses. It seemed that he started his Rolls Royce up before completely fastening the carburetor down and petrol leaked out, caught fire, and set a big rug on fire which was under the car, which spread through the attached garage and finally the whole house. His wife was out at the time, and she arrived just after me. Both were in a state of shock. They had lost everything! My colleague had only the work clothes he had on for repairing the car, so I gave him a full set of my clothes and after first consoling them, seeing them safely lodged in the next-door neighbor's house, I had no option but to drive all the way back to my hotel in Port Hawkesbury.

The following morning, the ship arrived in the Straits of Canso. We went out with the pilot to meet it. I was supposed to go on board with the pilot. The ship's crew threw a rope ladder over the side but would not stop the ship. The pilot went up first, swinging wildly, so wildly that he dropped his computer into the water. They then signaled for me to climb aboard, and I said, "Not bloody likely, I have had enough 'fun' for one trip!" Even then, going back in the pilot cutter, a whale breached and soaked us.

My former colleague pulled out his insurance policy which said $100,000, when his house would cost at least $300,000, to rebuild so he was very disheartened. He rang up the insurance company and they said, "Did you not read our letter of two months ago? We wrote to you to tell you we had increased your coverage to one million with no questions asked." He built a much bigger house on the same spot and rented a similar house while his was being rebuilt, all paid by the insurance company. Blessed assurance, the Prudential is mine!

Chapter 37:
China and Russia Again

Not long after that, I was sent to a conference in Moscow. My assistant had arranged a party for me, and I was picked up at the airport after coming off a plane Houston-New York-Moscow. I was whisked away in a large black Limo to a Dacha about ten miles from Moscow. When I got to the Dacha, a party was in full swing and on entering I was forced to drink the vodka toasts to all and sundry. Vodka and I do not get on! Within half an hour, I collapsed on the floor. They just left me there and continued to party over me saying, "He's one of us!" I came to six hours later with the Dacha deserted. It seems the Dacha owner was the former treasurer of the KGB and before that, the Dacha had been the home of the marshal of the Soviet Air Force who had been 'disposed of' in the Stalin purges of 1938. The house was then located next to the Kremlin but was moved in the 1950s.

The major power company in the UK where I had worked for many years decided to employ me as a consultant directly instead of through the American power company. One of the first tasks was to evaluate a start-up burner system. Their existing start-up burner system used heavy oil, but the tanks and pipework had been used initially for water, and by then the whole system was severely corroded with poor availability. They decided to look at a Chinese 'Coal Plasma' system being proposed by the boiler manufacturer.

My assistant, her daughter, and I flew to Hong Kong to visit the power plants there. I joined a team (six of us) and set off from Hong Kong to Yantai, China. Then we flew to Beijing, followed by Ho Hot Ho, Inner Mongolia. Yantai is a beach holiday resort on the Yellow Sea, but it is unlike most other beach resorts. The sand is covered by large tent structures with massive TV screens. During the day, the tents are packed with people, with nobody sunbathing or in the sea. When the sun goes down, there was a massive rush to get into the sea. I was told that the Chinese regard dark skin as inferior and do not want to darken their skin, and therefore do not expose themselves to the sun.

The test facility for this new plasma burner was set up in a school playground. We visited it during the day with school children playing in the yard. Even then it all looked strange, as the few trees which were there were black in color with no leaves. We were invited back at night for a test firing of the plasma burner when there were no school children present. Strangely, some fifty people were standing there carrying brushes and shovels.

They started up the system, and a jet of black powder enveloped all the people, including us and all the school playground. A few seconds later, they shut down the system and said, "Sorry, it was a misfire. We will try again." In those few seconds, we all gave the system, a "thumbs down"

The second time, it burst into life with a massive flame reaching thirty feet high, and we all jumped back! What it showed was the school yard, trees and buildings were black with coal dust from the first attempt as the fifty workmen went round trying to clean it up.

Afterward, we were also each presented with a box of the 'finest French Cabinet Sauvignon' wine grown in Yantai.

We thought about abandoning the rest of the trip but then thought, "What the hell? Let's just go sight-seeing." We got the chance to see all the sights of Beijing and visit the Great Wall. At Ho Hot Ho, Inner Mongolia, we were entertained by a singing and dancing group at an ethnic Mongolian dinner in a Yurt, and with my leadership replied with a rendering of 'Ilkley Moor Bat At' (a local folk song from near the major power company's base in the U.K.). The following day, we drove through miles and miles of coal heaps to the largest power plant in the world. All the staff used cars or bicycles, as it was three miles from one end of the boiler house to the other. They were using the plasma system and had a closed-circuit TV system monitoring every single burner. The smoke coming out of their chimneys was black, and they confidently explained their pollution systems were not in service as they used too much electricity.

With the help of an engineer at the large plant in the U.K., we wrote a paper entitled *The Reduction of Nitrous Oxides Emissions from Russian*

Coal. It was arranged for us to give a joint paper at a conference in St. Petersburg, Russia. I stayed at the hotel Europa, the best hotel in St. Petersburg on the banks of the Fan Tanka River, for the first three nights, as the conference was held in the Europa.

I met all my Russian friends, and we went out partying, especially to a bar/restaurant on the Fan Tanka River called the 'Purga', which means Blizzard in English. At this bar/restaurant, it is New Year's Eve every night of the week. We all drank cheap Russian Champagne, and I got so sloshed my assistant had to extricate me as I tried to pay the bill three times. She and two other girls had to carry me to a taxi.

I got up next day, worse for wear, to hear that my colleague from the power company, who I was supposed to give the paper with, would not be coming due to some disagreement with the Russian authorities. I had to recover quickly and learn his part of the paper, as I was presenting it that afternoon. I just rushed through his part of the paper so quickly the translators could not keep up with me and I dreaded any questions that might be asked. Somehow, I got through the presentation. Fortunately, a Turkish man got up, theoretically asking a question, but went rambling on about himself and his company, explaining how wonderful they were, and by the time he sat down everybody had had enough and I was saved from any more questions.

Chapter 38:
Round the World to Hawaii Again.

The main power company I was working for signed a contract to supply various qualities of coal from diverse sources with a power company in Hawaii. This involved conducting *one test a month*. I was occupied for an entire year, and unlike my first time on the islands, this was the most fun time of my whole career.

I normally travelled Varna-Budapest-Helsinki-Kyoto-Honolulu on the way there. Then I stayed seven days in Hawaii and then the journey back was a Honolulu-San Francisco-London-Varna, an 'around the world' flight ticket was the least expensive option at that time. To get this ticket, I had to stop at least two nights in either Budapest or Helsinki, two nights in Kyoto, two nights in San Francisco or London, as well seven days in Hawaii. This meant the round trip was a minimum of fifteen days but could be eighteen days due to the flight times. Once I arrived back in Varna, it was almost time to be off again round the world six to ten days later. It was great, partying in Helsinki, sometimes in Kyoto, Honolulu, and San Francisco or London!

On one occasion, the coal came from the Peace River area in Alberta, Canada and shipped via Prince Rupert, almost in Alaska. Much to everyone's astonishment, when the ship arrived, it was frozen solid... and this was in Hawaii! It seems that it snowed heavily on the stockpile and during ship loading at Prince Rupert. The coal had layers of ice (originally snow) like an ice cream sandwich.

The continuous ship unloader would not touch it, as the rubber buckets just skidded over the ice and coal. We had to use pneumatic chisels to be able to unload the coal and it took twenty days to get the coal off the ship. There was no point in flying back, so I just stayed there an extra five days on holiday.

I initially stayed at a Marriott Golf Resort, which overlooked the power plant on the southwest end of Oahu, but then moved to Waikiki where there was much more going on. From then on, I stayed in Waikiki and enjoyed the sun, sailing, and the nightlife.

One trip was over the summer solstices. One of the shift teams were going to celebrate overnight on top of a holly (to the Hawaiians) peak and invited me to go along. Unfortunately (or in hindsight, maybe fortunately), it was necessary to get written permission for 'outsiders' to go up this mountain, and permission was denied. It was for the best, as from their report's days after, the whole experience was drugs, drink, and sex, in that order.

My assistant came with me for one visit, and we did the usual round the world trip, stopping in Kyoto, Japan as it was cherry blossom time, then on to Hawaii. On the way back we stayed for three nights in San Francisco, two nights in Boston, and three nights in London before the flight back to Varna.

I went to the north coast one weekend with the idea of going surfing, but the waves were absolutely massive. Before I had even got on a board, walking down the beach, a very large wave rolled in shot up the beach and picked me up like a cork along with all the other people on the beach. It threw me some three hundred feet onto the main road next to my parked hire car, which ran at the top of the beach. I was lucky, since I was not injured and did not lose anything, but many others had broken bones or had lost everything to the wave: purses, car keys, shoes, and clothes. That was my one and only attempt at surfing in Hawaii.

I did the usual sights, visited South Sea Island village and Pearl Harbor, and walked up Diamond Head.

During my five extra days there, I was asked by the Hawaiian Power Company to go to the Big Island to look at a coal pile left some years ago to see if it was worthwhile recovering it. It was all covered in jungle and difficult to access, as well as being very near to the Kilauea Volcano, so of no interest. I got to go on a boat and see the lava streams entering the ocean and walk in the smoking Kilauea crater, but apart from that, it rained the whole time where I was, on the 'wet side' of the Big Island. What was funny was a bagpipe band, all in Hawaiian dress, playing traditional Scottish tunes in the pouring rain!

At the end of the twelve months, the Hawaiian contract was not renewed so that was the end of my Hawaiian adventures.

It was back to the U.K. again, and back to my involvement in multifuel tests including bituminous coal, sub-bituminous coal, and biomass. As some of these fuels were more reactive than bituminous coals, extra planning, safety reviews, and PPE were required.

The tests involved multiple organizations with some US 'experts.' One of these experts brought his twelve-bore shotgun with him, and he was immediately shown the door.

On one of the last trips we made to the largest plant in the U.K., we stayed as usual at the Marriott Hotel York. The weather turned nasty, and the River Ouse broke its banks and flooded the center of York. Middlegate Bridge was just about passable, but the famous Kings Staith Pub was under fifteen feet of water. What was worse was our favorite restaurant on the River Foss was underwater, and the side of the building collapsed into the river. So many good restaurants went out of business at that time.

The American Power company office in London decided to have an end of year party at one of my favorite places, Café De Paris. The party went with a real swing. One of the company employees came in his kilt and proceeded to show everyone what he had and had not got under his kilt. At our table was the CEO who was a bit of a wild person, six female staff members, and five other men. The CEO asked each woman in turn, "Of the men at this table, which one do you want to have sex with tonight and which one would you like to marry?" Only in Europe could you ask questions like that.

Chapter 39: Turkey

Following my exit from the oil company and during a lull of work for the power company, I was asked to assist a Turkish chemical company in building a power plant. They had contracted with a company in South Africa to design and build this power plant and wanted me to assist in the startup. They had contracted the South African company as they had built two other similar power plants using only cheap parts from decommissioned power plants. This is normally never done, but a low-cost power plant was what the Turkish company wanted.

I was invited to meet the owners at their headquarters in Istanbul and then visit the site of the power plant, which is at Yalova on the Asian side of the Marmara Sea. A driver took me the hundred or so miles from Istanbul to Yalova. The driver was an absolute lunatic, driving in heavy traffic at a hundred miles an hour. If the lanes were full of traffic, he just kept up the same speed on the *hard shoulder*, weaving across all the lanes. I have never been so frightened before.

There were no problems at the plant, and the staff seemed very Westernize except for the cleaners and the many *Chai Kuddies* (tea ladies) who all wore *hijab*. Whenever I sat down, anywhere on the plant, a glass of tea was put in front of me and always topped up.

A driver took me to the ferry in Yalova, which was supposed to take me to the ferry terminal in Istanbul where another driver would be waiting to take me back to the hotel in Taxim Square in the center of Istanbul. The driver in Yalova showed me the ferry and gave me a ticket. The ferry set off and arrived at a dock in the middle of nowhere and I was ordered to get off. The driver had put me on the wrong ferry! I had no Turkish Lira and spoke no Turkish, but fortunately had my mobile phone with me, so I phoned the plant manager in Yalova. He realized I was on the wrong ferry and told me to hunt for a taxi, which were few and far between, and hand the drive my mobile and let the plant manager speak to him. Four hours later, we arrived at the hotel who were waiting for us, and the hotel manager came out and paid the taxi driver.

Starting the work, my assistant and I drove from Kranevo, which in itself was an adventure. The route to the plant was torturous: a difficult route to drive to Burgas, and then an almost non-existent track, even though it was designated E 87 through route, from Burgas to Malko Turnovo at 3,000 feet, just before the border where we stayed the night. As we had to catch the car ferry from Yenikapi (in the center of Istanbul), to Yalova at 1 pm, we had to be up at the crack of dawn to get through the border crossing and drive the 160 miles to the ferry. Invariably there was a party going on at the one and only hotel in Mako Turnovo, so it was difficult to get an early night's sleep.

The border crossing could be tricky, with the car being searched. There were numerous line-ups for checking the car papers, passports, visas, and toll sticker at the Bulgarian side, and on the Turkish side as we were leaving the European Union. Fortunately, they had just completed (and I mean *just*, as there were stones on the highway giving us a puncture) the six-lane road from the border to Istanbul, and there was little traffic the first 60 miles. In parts, we had the road to ourselves, but the police had it to themselves, too. The traffic in Istanbul was crazy, with people driving at 100 miles an hour and many accidents, the most major with fatalities. The police just moved them, including bodies, to one side of the road and allowed the traffic to keep moving.

It was just possible to get to the ferry in time and another car search for the trip across the Marmara Sea to Yalova in Asia. We were put up in a hotel called the 'Elegance', but also in the company's own motel called the AKMOTEL. The hotel was always full of Saudi Arabians. Their women went in the swimming pool in full Chador.

Wine was very expensive and difficult to obtain at the hotel. No wine was available at the motel. There was only one English TV channel, Aljazeera.

For this plant, the first boiler came from South Africa. The second boiler, from Poland, had been built twenty years earlier but never put in use. The turbines were one from South Africa and one from the Czech Republic and were both 1960s vintage. Other parts were from Austria and were only a few years old when Austria stopped burning coal, or Germany, France, and the UK The Turkish company had never built or been involved in a power plant before. I must admit, I thought the idea crazy, and it would not work.

I joined the project as the foundations of the plant were being poured. No sooner had the foundations been poured when the South African company went bankrupt, and I was left to carry on the project on my own with the totally inexperienced Turkish engineers. I was really surprised. They made many mistakes but were really quick to realize their mistakes and moved heaven and earth to correct them. Some mistakes which I thought would take months to correct, they corrected in a week. Not only were they adaptive learners, they were dynamic, and all worked as a single team. They thought nothing about working for twenty-four hours at a stretch to solve a problem.

The work was tough and needed concentration 24/7. They thought I should dedicate my life to their plant, which I could not do. We spent at least one week at the plant every month for two years. At least we got to visit all the historical sites in northern Asiatic Turkey and Istanbul. They had their Muslim holidays, but they got really upset when I asked for Christmas day off.

The workers did not take care of delicate electrical equipment and stripped off the protective coverings and left them out in the dust and rain. I was sure the plant would never work, but to my surprise, it started up and operated without a hitch.

Altogether, they were a great bunch of people and except for keeping the Muslim holidays there were little or no religious restrictions, including drinking alcohol and fraternizing between sexes. By the time the plant was up and running, the police started to enforce lower motorway and road speeds with masses of speed cameras and heavy fines. This increased the time to get to the border from the plant, as it caused long tailbacks of traffic.

Chapter 40: My Big Birthday

Normally, I went to Houston from mid-January to mid-March, giving me time to celebrate my three grandchildren's birthdays, as well as my own. But in that particular year, I had too much work in Europe to do that. I thought of going back to the states for my big birthday, but work intervened, and I could not get there. I did not intend missing it without a party, so in the end, I had four parties.

The power company I was working for asked me to get involved in coal from Indonesia to the Philippines. The original idea was that I would go to Indonesia, watch the ship being loaded with coal, and then travel on the ship to the plant in the Philippines and then be there for the test of the coal. The big issue was insurance: who would give me personal insurance and who would pay for it? The passage from Indonesia to the Philippines was fraught with modern-day pirates in fast boats who made a habit of holding people to ransom. In the end, nobody could agree who would carry the insurance, and it forced me to change my plans.

I had friends in St. Petersburg who wanted to spend my birthday with me, so I set out on the following trip. Varna (Bulgaria)-Budapest (Hungary)-Helsinki (Finland)-Singapore-Balikpapan (Indonesia)-Singapore-Manila-Masinloc-Manila (all Philippines)-Bangkok (Thailand)-Helsinki-Budapest-Varna. I stopped in Helsinki for one night and partied with friends who travelled from St. Petersburg, Russia and Helsinki. I then went on and stopped in Singapore for one night and flew to Balikpapan the next day. The amazing thing in Balikpapan was to see over-loaded coal barges coming down the river and almost sinking, with the coal drowned in water and being loaded onto the ship. I flew back to Singapore after the ship was loaded, but then I had four days to wait somewhere while the ship arrived in the Philippines. I decided to stay in Singapore after my earlier problems in the Philippines. I did the usual sites, and on my last night in Singapore visited a tourist bar on the riverfront.

Next to me sat two girls who said they were from Thailand. They were working for an immigration service company and were travelling to various capitals in Southeast Asia. They asked me where I was going next, and I told them that I was flying to Manila in the morning. To my surprise they said, "Oh so are we. Which flight are you on?" and guess what? They were on the same flight as me! They then asked which hotel I was staying at and how long I would be there. Lo and behold, I was staying at the same hotel as they were staying, but then I was only staying one night and then going upcountry for six days. They then asked when I was flying back to Singapore, and I told them I wasn't, as I was flying to Bangkok seven days later.

They then said, "Oh we are also flying back to Bangkok that day on Thai airways at 10 am! Which flight are you on?" You guessed it, the same flight! How could this be? It was too much of a coincidence! They then asked, "Which hotel are you staying at in Bangkok?"

I said, "Well, none, I am staying in between the airport and Pattaya twelve miles south of Bangkok as I have a very early morning flight to Helsinki," to which they replied, "Good, we will drive you there, see you tomorrow on the plane!"

Uhhhhhh...

From Manila, I was taken upcountry to a hotel in Subic Bay by a maniac driver. The hotel was clean, and it seemed I was the only person in the hotel. Subic Bay, which used to be a large U.S. navy base, is a ghost town now. Following the eruption of Mount Pinatubo, the U.S. navy left Subic Bay as well as Clark Airforce base on the opposite site of Pinatubo. At dinner, I was the only one present, and had an orchestra to myself.

The whole area round there had been devastated by the eruption. The rivers became completely silted up with white volcanic ash, and the river's course, in some cases, took a shortcut to the sea, washing away many houses and in some cases whole villages.

The following morning, I was driven the hour and a half to Masinloc where I saw the ship had arrived. At the plant, they were getting ready for the test. Some Americans and Norwegians working there ask why I was staying in Subic Bay as there was a hotel near the plant in Masinloc where all the expats were staying.

I agreed to move hotels. Ahh. We have been here before! There was a knock at the door, and a 'temporary wife' waiting. All the expats had temporary wives. I spent five days there, even travelling by water-buffalo taxi, and then the frightful journey by car back to Manila airport.

Sure enough, there were the two Thai girls waiting for me. From the plane, they took me by car to my hotel. We had dinner, and I bade them farewell just after midnight on my birthday. Very early that morning, I flew back to Helsinki and met some more of my Russian St. Petersburg friends, and we celebrated my birthday as it was still my birthday due to the time change. Still, had to go to bed as I had been up twenty-eight hours already that day. The next day, I flew Helsinki-Budapest-Varna, and had another birthday party in Varna! By then, I was well and truly beat!

My last trip to the Philippines was on behalf of an Indonesian company, and my Bulgarian assistant came too (to keep an eye on me and keep records). They had had an explosion at the plant, and I was supposed to find out the route cause and propose solutions. The plant is on the famous Bataan Peninsula, which is new and being massively extended by a famous international beer brewing company. I was not impressed by the coal they bought, as it was a low heating value lignite and was almost completely dust by the time it got to the plant. It was like going into a dust bowl, and the engineers had really no idea what they were dealing with. I decided that I'd had enough at the plant, and I told them the truth about their plant and that it was a death trap. They agreed.

I was instructed to author a report in graphic form to the Chief Executive Officer who had flown into Manila from Mexico City, supposedly to hear my report. The brewing company decided I should present my findings at a lavish dinner in one of the best hotels in Manila, close to their Manila headquarters. Giving a presentation during a lavish dinner is far from ideal, especially when I told them "You should keep brewing beer and not get involved in power generation!"

We were met with stony silence until they muttered, "Send us your report." We were not shown the door.

That is the beauty of the end of a career: You don't have to brown-nose!

I recommended major changes in design (which I knew they would not accept). The sting in the tail was the company only paid me half of my invoice, with the Indonesian government withholding a further twenty percent. They actually asked me to do some work for them again, but I doubled my fee which they did not accept, so I withdrew all offers to work with them again.

Chapter 41.
Inhospitable project locations.

Projects in relatively peaceful locations had by now dried up and only ones in difficult, dangerous places required my assistance. I started to wonder if it was time to 'throw in the towel.'

A new plant was under construction in the Ganges River delta in Bangladesh, and the operators needed some training. The plant was being built and funded by the Chinese under their 'Road and Bridge' program. All the engineers, management and craftsmen were Chinese with unskilled manual workers being all Bangladeshi. The working language for the start-up of the plant was supposed to be English but very few of the Chinese or the local Bangladeshi people were fluent in English which caused significant friction right from the start of the project.

The plant was only accessible at certain times, as the river was often flooded and anyone arriving on site, they could get stranded for weeks. Even without flooding, the travel from Dakar, the capitol of Bangladesh, was difficult, and required taking three ferries and driving more than one hundred miles over rough roads. Still, I prepared to go there.

Just before my planned departure, I learned that I would be saved the trouble. A major event occurred when the Bangladeshi workers killed a Chinese craftsman from the company building the plant. A whole full-scale riot broke out, resulting in more deaths and the army having to be brought in to separate the warring factions. That ended my interest in the project.

The company in London had got involved with a nickel plant in Guatemala. This plant was located deep in the jungle some 40 miles from Puerto Barrios on the east coast of Guatemala and was owned by a Russia nickel company with only Russian employees. The plant was like an island with only a single-track dirt road connecting the workers to the outside world. We were told it had a disused air strip near the plant, and they were having problems and had blown up one of their boilers. They were hopeful that we could help solve their problems.

We traveled from Sofia to Guatemala City via Madrid, Spain, and Panama City. Following a meeting in Guatemala City where we met the manager from the company in London, we stayed at Antigua, the ancient capital of Spanish America, for three days. Antigua is full of colonial Spanish buildings and, traditions and even the people are very more Spanish in looks and attitude than other Amer-Indian town and villages. During out visit there were massive colorful religious processions. Antigua is situated at 3000 feet above sea level with a relatively mild climate between two active volcanos which were belching out gas and some lava.

The original idea was to drive the 170 miles to the plant, but we were warned that the road to the plant bisected immigrate routes from El Salvador through Guatemala and Mexico to the southern boarder of the USA. Not only were the half-starved immigrants a problem but there were marauding bands, praying on the immigrates and on anybody else who traveled on that road. If you were lucky, you would just get robbed; if you were unlucky, you would not be seen again.

We searched around and found a small plane and pilot who had landed on the strip before, and with the help of contacts in Guatemala, paid in advance. On the flight, we had a wonderful view of the volcanic eruptions. The air strip was almost closed in by the jungle, but the pilot successfully landed. We were greeted by *nobody*. No sign of life, except for alligators in the creek surrounding the strip.

An hour later, a beaten-up truck arrived to take us to the plant. The plant was drastically short of finance and in a poor state. The people at the plant, including managers, staff, engineers, and even manual workers were all Russia, surly and miserable. We were totally ignored; it was like we were invisible to them. My assistant who spoke Russian fluently had difficulty getting them to converse. It wasn't that they did not like us; my assistant found out the people hated being there and just wanted to leave and go anywhere else. They regarded it as worse than prison. Some of them had not been paid in months or been home in years and felt totally abandoned.

At least the coal was stored indoors as it is an area of high precipitation. The boilers and plant were not designed by any reputable company, and it seemed like everything was just thrown together. It needed a massive investment program to ensure efficient, economically effective plant operation, and there seemed little or no likelihood of any investment at all.

Gradually the employees became happier to talk but they just kept grumbling with no positive feelings at all. At the end of the day, we were happy to get back on the plane but also somewhat sad to see competent people suffering hardship.

Nobody was going to fund a project to even assess their problems never mind layout recommendations and solutions, so we all walked away from it.

We flew back Guatemala City to Atlanta, then to Amsterdam and back to Sofia. In Atlanta, I assumed that with my American passport, it would get me through immigration faster than my assistant who had an American visa. After immigration, I waited and waited but there was no sign of her. I thought I had time to get to the plane to Amsterdam but got to the gate just as the plane was leaving the stand. It seemed my assistant had got through immigration even faster than me and was on the plane. Fortunately for me, there was another plane to Amsterdam two hours later and as we had a three-hour connecting time in Amsterdam, I was still able to catch my last flight to Sofia without too much difficulty.

Chapter 42: The Big Full Stop

As the environmental requirements became tighter, my work with coal became less, and what little work there was involved changing fuels to less nitrous oxide-polluting fuels. I worked on plants like Avon Lake, Baltimore to change their source from Bituminous coal to sub-bituminous coal, which by then was only operating when there was an exceptionally high demand for electricity. Over the period June 2002 to December 2019, I had six retirement parties. The last one was in London, where thirty of my colleagues came from different parts of the world. At this party, they took a vote on whether I should write a book of my adventures, and the vote was twenty-nine for one against. That one was me.

Even in December 2019, there was still no major issue with CO_2, and I was persuaded to continue working. March 12th, 2020 was my birthday. Immediately after I was to fly to Calgary for three days followed by a flight to Istanbul and on to Sofia, and a further two days later fly to Liverpool for a week. I drove to Houston George

Bush airport and went to the airline desk who said, "The flight to Calgary is operating, but the return flight is cancelled due to Covid, as are all the flights out of Canada. If you go on the flight, you will be quarantined in Calgary for two weeks and then you will have no way of returning to Houston."

I said, "Thanks for the information, but I will not be flying with you."

I finally was able to return to Bulgaria in June but then got isolated in quarantine for two weeks, and since then business travel has been out of the question. Between March 2020 and September 2021, a storm blew in concerning CO_2 emissions, which seemed to dominate the news with various environmental groups making sit-ins and blocking off not only power plants, but roads, too, and screaming "Dirty coal!" In view of this, I became more involved in biomass and even RDF-Refuse Derived Fuel. In September 2021, the price of coal rocketed to $230/ton, due to the shortage of natural gas, while the price of cleaned garbage pellets fell to NEGATIVE $60/ton. There is an absolute fortune to be made for anybody who can successfully use garbage in a boiler designed for coal firing.

Following Vladimir Putin's invasion of the Ukraine, life has got even more hectic. The demand, especially in Eastern Europe, for any sort of fuel has soared and everybody and anybody has been rushed into action to find alternative fuels to Russian gas. Environmental concerns are on the 'back burner' for now.

As well as that, Kranevo has now some 4,000 Ukrainian refugees all of who are in a state of shock and bewilderment. They are housed in the tourist hotels for now but what happens come summer?

A dynamic situation and you may know the answer by now!

Covid dee, Covid da, life goes on, bah ha!

La la, la la, life goes on!

The owner of Viking cruise line, in an advert shown often on TV says: "I have never regretted what I have done, my only regretted is what I have not done."

I wish I could say the same. I will let you work out what I regret.